'Terror and Pity reign in every Breast'

Gothic Drama in the London Patent Theatres, 1750–1820

Paul Ranger

THE SOCIETY FOR THEATRE RESEARCH

First published 1991
by The Society for Theatre Research
c/o The Theatre Museum, 1E Tavistock Street,
Covent Garden, London WC2E 7PA

Cover illustration (see p. 68) reproduced by
permission of Sheffield Art Galleries

Typeset by BP Integraphics Ltd, Bath, Avon
Printed in Great Britain by The Bath Press, Avon

Contents

Acknowledgements

This work stems from my doctoral thesis on the gothic researched under the supervision of Mr James L. Smith and Professor John Smith at the University of Southampton. I would like to acknowledge gratefully the guidance I received from them. Thanks must go too to my employers at that time, King Alfred's College, Winchester, for grants and study leave.

Invaluable help has been afforded by the staff of the Bodleian Library, Bristol University Theatre Collection, the British Library, the British Museum, the Folger Shakespeare Library, the Harvard Theatre Collection, Hereford Public Library and Museum, King Alfred's College Library, the Royal Archives, the archive of the Royal Opera House, the Theatre Museum and the Victoria and Albert Museum.

I am grateful to Dr Pieter van der Merwe for reading the draft of this book and for his detailed advice on the presentation of the work. It is a great pleasure to thank Mr George Speaight for his editorial expertise and for his enthusiastic encouragement of the project.

Lastly I must thank the spectres of those many performers who for a while made the gothic drama a reality on the London stage. Without them there would be no story.

Paul Ranger
Oxford

Preface

This book is an examination of the gothic drama in performance. Much could be written about aspects other than staging – but not here!

However infrequently a play was mounted, even if it received but a single performance, it qualifies as an exemplificatory text for the purposes of this work. Of course, many an eighteenth-century play was only tolerated for a single airing and then dismissed. At the first mention of each play the date of the initial London production is given. Many of the plays entered the repertoire of provincial companies but reference has been made to the country theatres only in as much as remarks about productions clarify the practices at the two metropolitan patent houses, the Theatres Royal at Covent Garden and Drury Lane.

A limitation has been imposed on the span of time which the work encompasses: the years 1750 until 1820 form the period under surveillance. This has allowed several early gothic plays such as John Home's *Douglas* and Arthur Murphy's *The Grecian Daughter* to be included. The latter date may seem to be an arbitrary one when seen in relation to events in Britain and Europe but after that year no new ground was broken in the presentation of gothic plays, although one or two interesting spectacles were put on as 'out of due time'.

Throughout the book the emphasis is on the practicalities of staging the plays, an activity which drew on the skills of playwrights, acting managers, performers, musicians, designers and machinists. Every play was staged for the enjoyment of the audience and so the response of its members is important. Other than these reactions, no evaluation of the plays has been attempted. How could we judge the gothic dramas today? They are no longer performed in the London theatres, we cannot see the spectacles they once offered, nor have we the sensibilities of a Georgian audience. Hence it seems important to reconstruct these dramas of the past and allow the reader to make his own response to the entertainment.

Our expectation is well worked up and Terror and Pity reign in every Breast, till by due Degrees the Discovery is made, when a Tide of Joy breaks in upon us . . .

London Chronicle, 12–15 March 1757

George Richard Pain's painting of the Castle of Otranto (signed 1831) exaggerates the gothic motifs – louring clouds, a vast barren landscape and an amassed jumble of towers – Walpole employed in describing the setting of his novel. (*Clarendon Gallery.*)

Chapter One: The Gothic Spirit

Neither eighteenth-century playwrights, nor members of their audiences, used the term 'a gothic drama'. It was a label applied by literary critics only with hindsight to certain types of play. Instead, words suggesting the form rather than the content described the work. Thus the *St James's Chronicle* referred to *The Castle Spectre* (Matthew Gregory Lewis, 1797) as 'a drama of a mingled nature, Operatic, Comical and Tragical' and at greater length the *Morning Chronicle* defined George Colman the Younger's play, *Feudal Times* (1799), as 'an exhibition of music and dialogue, pantomime and dancing, painting and machinery, antique dresses and armour, thunder and lightning, fire and water...'[1] Yet in spite of this variety of form, there was an homogeneity about the content that prompts one to question why certain scenes or stock devices repeatedly appeared. An establishment of the common ground held by a multiplicity of plays categorised as 'gothic' would eventually be a help in arriving at an understanding of this term.

In the prologue to *The Castle Spectre* Lewis suggested a starting point for this exploration. He used the figure of Romance to introduce his listeners to a number of specific locations which he would deem to be gothic:

> She loathes the sun, or blazing taper's light;
> The moon-beam'd landscape and tempestuous night
> Alone she loves; and oft, with glimmering lamp,
> Near graves new-open'd, or midst dungeons damp,
> Drear forests, ruin'd aisles, and haunted towers,
> Forlorn she roves, and raves away the hours![2]

I

In his list of church-yards, dungeons, forests, ruined churches, castles – all locations frequently used by the gothic playwright – Lewis was harking back to Samuel Johnson's dictionary definition of the word 'Romantick': 'wild . . . improbable; false . . .; fanciful; full of wild scenery'.[3] Lewis wrote an epilogue to Thomas Holcroft's play, *Knave or Not* (1798) in which he added to the list of locations some of the other appurtenances of the gothic:

> Give us Lightning and Thunder, Flames, Daggers and Rage;
> With events that ne'er happened, except on the Stage;
> When your Spectre departs, through a trapdoor ingulph her,
> Burn under her nose, too, some brimstone and sulpher.

Miles Peter Andrews, in his preface to the publication of the songs in *The Enchanted Castle* (1786), listed other elements he had detected in similar entertainments:

> The Clank of Chains, the Whistling of Hollow Winds, the Clapping
> of Doors, Gigantic Forms, and visionary Gleams of Light . . .[4]

Not all playwrights banished these listings to prologues and epilogues. The gothic motifs were so integral to the plot that the audience's attention was drawn to them in the course of the action as John O'Keeffe did in *The Castle of Andalusia* (1782): standing in the moonlight outside the castle of the title, Don Caesar, the leader of the banditti, sang of the baying wolf, the midnight hour, shrieking females and maurauding brigands. To modern readers it appears that playwrights were setting out markers surrounding the gothic territory in which the action was to be placed.[5]

Eighteenth-century novelists had fused location and action more securely for the lengthier form in which they worked. Unencumbered by the necessity to compress a story into the couple of hours allowed to the playwright, writers took the opportunity to present themes of darkness in an expanded and integrated fashion. Many would nominate Horace Walpole's romance, *The Castle of Otranto*, as the seminal gothic novel.[6] On the banks of the Thames at Twickenham Walpole had created a miniature gothic castle, a fantasy which served as the backdrop of his own self-conscious existence. At first no more than a cottage, 'the prettiest bauble' said Walpole, his domain eventually boasted a library, the Round Tower, the Holbein Bedroom and the Great Cloister, whilst still retaining the bijou quality of the original building. Within, a warm darkness pervaded which Walpole termed 'gloomth'.[7] Here Walpole wrote his chivalric romance, a tale of strange, supernatural events. But whereas the details of his real castle, Strawberry Hill, were neat and contained, Otranto was conceived on a vast scale, the stage for colourful processions and tournaments. Both castles were alike in their enveloping gloom ('Take away that light,' shouted Manfred, demonstrating the villain's hatred of the clear light of day); alike, too, in their respective owners' love of the odd and the incongruous, and in the impression given that both buildings were likely environments in which to await supernatural visitants.[8] Walpole's own phobias were writ large in *Otranto* so that they might terrify the reader, – the giant feathers on the expanding helmet which killed the young Conrad for example.

Terror was an important constituent in the gothic novel. The literary landscape which the essayists John Aikin and Anna Barbauld viewed was one strewn with such catastrophes as murders, shipwrecks, fires and earthquakes, all events with which the gothic playwrights were familiar. A 'gothic fragment' by the two writers was set in the ruins of a 'large antique mansion' on which a storm beat while hollow groans resounded in the subterranean vault. The effect of these circumstances was, claimed the authors, to elevate 'the soul to its highest pitch', again as much an aim of the playwright as the novelist.[9] With such works in mind, George Colman light-heartedly summed up the constituents of the gothic novel:

> A novel, now, is nothing more
> Than an old castle and a creaking door:
> A distant hovel –
> Clanking of chains – a gallery – a light –
> Old armour – and a phantom all in white –
> And there's a novel.[10]

The writer who fashioned similar settings and circumstances into lengthy, involved works of art was Ann Radcliffe. For her the landscape was of paramount importance; through it her heroines were perpetually journeying from one great house to another. Although her settings were less overtly horrific than the Aikin-

Barbauld scenery, Radcliffe supplied for dramatists many a castle in ruins, underrun by secret passages, rotting in a wild, brigand-infested landscape:

> This was a scene as *Salvator* would have chosen, had he then existed, for his canvas; St Aubert, impressed by the romantic character of the place, almost expected to see banditti start from behind some projecting rock, and he kept his hand upon the arms with which he always travelled.'[11]

No wonder that her novels found adaptors prepared to transmute them to the stage.

All of the gothic plays were set in the past, the past of an indeterminate, quasi-mediaeval Europe. Precision may have seemed pedantic. Walpole, after the publication of *The Castle of Otranto*, wrote to William Cole that his mind was filled with 'Gothic story' and the preface to the first edition stated that the action took place between the first and the last of the Crusades; in other words, between 1095 and 1243, a leeway of over one hundred and fifty years.[12] Clara Reeve, who, after Walpole, wrote a similar tale of chivalry in which a process of rationalisation was applied to supernatural events, forebore to make a precise statement about the period of her work, instead referring to it as a 'picture of Gothic times and manners'.[13] The term was used as an indication of atmosphere, rather than as a reference to given dates. When gothic works were staged this vagueness was an occasion of difficulty for the scene and costume designers, as well as leaving the audience with the impression that it was suspended in an indeterminate time-scale. A writer in the *Critical Review*, after seeing Andrew MacDonald's play, *Vimonda* (1787), summed up this feeling of disorientation:

> Events are supposed to have taken place in the days of chivalry: a word with which we constantly connect the idea of something wild and extravagant.[14]

Many spectators, however, simply accepted the vagueness. After the first night of *The Haunted Tower* (James Cobb, 1789) the *Prompter* reported that history had 'nothing to do with the groundwork of this Opera'.[15] That admission made, there was no further reference to infelicities in the presentation of the past, for the interest of the audience lay in the characters and situations. The activities of these characters reflected not the actions of folk in mediaeval moralities and mysteries so much as the deeds of the dark characters of Jacobean and Caroline tragedy. Indeed, the later plays of Shakespeare and the blood-suffused dramas of Thomas Otway were highly popular in the latter part of the eighteenth century and their atmosphere seeped into the gothic.

Not until the stage management of John Philip Kemble, with his antiquarian interest demanding correct and detailed settings, aided by his scene designer, William Capon, was the visual element of the gothic drama presented with historical accuracy. Capon scrupulously kept drawing books of London's mediaeval and Tudor buildings which served as the basis for the scenes he painted in his large studio.[16] Viewing the progress, in addition to Kemble, would be men such as James Boaden, the editor of the *Oracle*, and Sir Joshua Reynolds who commended, wrote Boaden, 'the accuracy and bold execution' of these 'scenes of past ages'.[17] The result of this accurate visual portrayal should have been to root the plays in an historical truth, but this eluded most of the audience. Applause was for the spectacular nature of Capon's settings, not their veracity.

More attention was, however, paid to an accuracy in the representation of the geographical settings for the concept of place is more tangible than that of time. Thomas Gray was but one of many writers who kept careful notes of tours, whether to the Lake District or further afield.[18] The upkeep of a travel diary with its detailed descriptions of scenes and the accounts of the author's response provided an important literary souvenir. These diaries were far from private: each traveller aimed to publish his thoughts, giving to library shelves such works as the Revd William Gilpin's various sets of observations made whilst in the highlands of Scotland, Richard Warner's prose account of his ramble through Wales and William Sotheby's verse compilation on the sights of the principality. Farther from home the Revd William Coxe kept an account of his travels in the Alps and Ann Radcliffe commented on her visit to Holland and Germany. This established habit of travellers putting pen to paper prompted Joseph Cradock to remark:

As every one who has either traversed a steep mountain, or crossed
a small channel, must write his Tour, it would be almost unpardonable
in Me to be totally silent, who have visited the most uninhabitable
regions of North Wales...[19]

Both playwrights and novelists made reference to this literary
corpus which tended to improve the accuracy of scenic descriptions.
Mrs Radcliffe's Emily journeyed from one castle to another in
The Mysteries of Udolpho surveying and responding to the wild
scenery of her travels. Conversations, too, were full of the talk
of scenery: as Valancourt conversed with Emily 'there was often
a tremulous tenderness in his voice, and sometimes he expatiated
on [the scenes] with all the fire of genius'.[20] Even when Emily
reached her several destinations she would stand by the open casement gazing at the 'wild grandeur of the scene, closed nearly on
all sides by alpine steeps, whose tops, peering over each other,
faded from the eye in misty hues...'[21] Nevertheless, the landscape
did not exist in its own right but as part of the heroine's consciousness. Aesthetically it upheld her, although its benignity was sometimes at variance with the roughness of the terrain.

Gothic romances served as a source for playwrights and the
detailed visual backgrounds were helpful in creating settings in
the text. They were equally helpful to the scene designer in his
attempts to provide a setting for the play. James Boaden, for
instance, took another of Radcliffe's novels, *The Italian*, which
he used as the basis for his play, *The Italian Monk* (1797). The
descriptions of the lush Italian countryside found their echo in
the dialogue. But they were doubly used, for Gaetano Marinari,
the Haymarket's scene painter, was in a position to use both the
playwright's stage-directions, as well as the novelist's accounts of
prospects and architecture, in creating the settings for the play.[22]

Painters travelled, as well as writers, recording in water-colour
scenes which later were to be worked into easel paintings. The
notes made on one of Philippe Jacques de Loutherbourg's tours
of the county of Derby were used as a series of scenes for an entertainment at Drury Lane entitled *The Wonders of Derbyshire* (1779),
in which such concrete images as a view of Matlock, Chatsworth
House and Gardens and the caverns of Castleton anchored the
entertainment in a factual depiction of specific locations.[23] The

sketch-books of another scene painter, Michael 'Angelo' Rooker, reveal his detailed interest in such subjects as castles, the ruins of abbeys at Netley, Llanthony and Glastonbury and a variety of townscapes. It was this keen observation which gained commendation for his stage depictions of such locations as St James's Park, Portsmouth illuminated for victory celebrations and the view of London from Highgate Ponds.[24] Designers tended to resort to clichés in their over-easy presentation of castle and convent interiors. Then the audience found the stock scenes or rapid knock-ups unconvincing. On the other hand, specific townscapes were a challenge to which designers rose with aplomb. The portrayal of the Grand Square in Moscow in Frederick Reynolds's play, *The Exile* (1808), was greeted with acclaim by the critic in the *European Magazine* and it had earlier praised extravagantly the view of Orleans seen at dawn in *Valentine and Orson* (Thomas Dibdin, 1804).[25]

In some respects the work of the stage designer was comparable with that of the garden designer in the eighteenth century for both attempted to create a scene which would induce in the spectator an emotional response. The visitor to the theatre had merely to sit and watch the progression of the scenes but the visitor to the garden was responsible for his own progression from one setting to another. In this he was guided by a circuit walk from which vistas opened before him; he also entered a series of enclosed spaces, each designed to elicit an emotional response: a prospect might arouse in him feelings of cheerfulness and alternatively the cool darkness of a cypress grove would fill him with quiet melancholy. This changing pattern of emotion was described in Richard Graves's novel *The Spiritual Quixote* in the commentary on Mr Rivers's garden. It was

> laid out in a romantic taste with a proper mixture of the allegro and the penseroso, the cheerful and the gloomy: tufts of roses, jasmines and the most fragrant flowering shrubs, with a serpentine walk of cypresses and laurels, here and there an urn, with suitable inscriptions, and terminated by a rough arch of rock work that covered a dripping fountain, were its principal beauties.[26]

In the garden of fiction the novelist created the responses. The factual garden could drawn responses just as surely, as is evident from Humphrey Repton's selection of adjectives in his account

The Vale of Venus at Rousham, Oxfordshire, designed by William Kent; at this stage the circuit walk is merely hinted at. (*C. Cottrell-Dormer, Esq., Rousham; Courtauld Institute of Art.*)

of a visit to Downton Castle, Richard Payne Knight's estate in Herefordshire:

> A narrow, wild and natural path sometimes creeps under the beetling rock, close by the margin of a mountain stream. It sometimes ascends to an awful precipice, from whence the foaming waters are heard roaring in the dark abyss below, or seen wildly dashing against its opposite banks; while in other places, the course of the river being impeded by natural ledges of rock, the vale presents a calm, glassy mirror, that reflects the surrounding foliage.[27]

Repton contrasted awe and calmness, each induced by a separate prospect. Melancholy was envisaged as the heart's cleanser and frequent opportunities were given to savour it in Alexander Pope's garden at Twickenham, which contained a gloomy grotto, dusky groves and, as a climax at the end of a grove of cypresses, the tomb of the poet's mother.[28] This stress gave truth to Walpole's dictum that it was 'always comic to set aside a quarter of one's garden to be melancholy in'.[29] Sheer terror could also be encoun-

tered in these garden scenes. On a visit to China, Sir William
Chambers noted an oriental gothic garden:

> Their scenes of terror are composed of gloomy woods, deep valleys
> inaccessible to the sun, impending barren rocks, dark caverns, and
> impetuous cataracts rushing down the mountains from all parts ...
> Bats, owls, vultures, and every bird of prey flutter in the groves; wolves,
> tigers and jackals howl in the forests ...[30]

He went on to tell of the inscribed stones set up in the garden
which recorded barbarous acts perpetrated by brigands on the land
over which the visitor passed. Chambers used the term 'scene' in
describing these prospects.[31] In this he was not alone. Thomas
Whatley, gazing at one of the views at Hagley in Worcestershire,
commended it as a 'perfect opera scene' and Repton contrasted
the scene which the theatre-goer viewed with that of the garden
visitor noting that the artist's use of perspective gave value to the
theatrical scene, a technique of which the garden design was deprived.[32] Whether the scene was in the garden or the theatre it
was designed to induce an emotional response in the beholder.
Mention has already been made of those features in a garden which
produced a feeling of melancholy. Other scenes would produce
different responses: wild crags and a cascade of water could strike
terror, a fear that the place was the lair of the banditti and yet,
on the other hand, an open prospect of hills and clumped trees
could impart serenity.[33] Some of the responses were, of course,
conventionalised but playwrights nevertheless made use of
emotional settings in order to hint at the action which was to follow
allowing the mood of the scene to be anticipated in advance.

A formal appreciation of landscape painting, a privilege which
educated members of the audience enjoyed, helped to foster discern-
ment in viewing scenery. The eighteenth-century's most highly
collectable painters were three artists active in the previous century,
the Neapolitan, Salvator Rosa, and two French painters, Claude
Lorraine and Nicolas Poussin.

> Whate'er Lorraine light-touched with soft'ning hue,
> Or savage Rosa dashed, or learned Poussin drew ...

wrote James Thomson in *The Castle of Indolence.* All three men
influenced landscape design and thereby, indirectly, stage design.

The paintings of Claude gave one a long vista of receding planes, as if the scene was composed of wings and back-drop. In the distance mountains and wild forests were just discernible and as the planes advanced to the foreground one was conscious of the force of natural elements: the gushing river, the waterfall, wild trees twisted into a series of frames to surround the prospect, all contrasted with the order of classical buildings, quays and the commerce of mankind. We have already noticed the awe with which eighteenth-century travellers viewed the natural setting. This was suggested in the landscapes of Claude but in those of Rosa it was more than suggested – it was exaggerated. For Rosa the natural scene was untamed and the hastily applied impasto on his canvas revealed his own response to the landscape. His scenes were dark but camp fires or the full moon highlighted the brigands and uncouth shepherds who inhabited the wild hills of his fevered imagination.

The landscapes of the gothic dramas became conventionalised; castles were always ruinous, forests set in deep gloom and the sea-shore lashed by the storm-driven waves. Their stock nature enabled the theatre-goer to recognise the gothic quality of a play and it was only to be expected that stock characters would perform within these locations.

Visitors to the playhouse could expect to see the clearly delineated stock characters of the romantic hero and heroine; the villain, a personification of relentless greed or self-devouring jealousy and the divided hero, a man at odds with himself who, through some insidious fault, crumbled before the spectators' eyes. In contrast to these major characters, lighter entertainment was provided by a bevy of humorous domestics or rustics whose lives were lived on a different emotional plane than that of the intense and passionate breathings of their superiors.

The conventional quality of each role allowed actors to specialise and for each type certain qualities were needed. A singing voice was a requisite for the part of the youthful hero. A sturdy figure and a bass voice through which a range of disturbed passions could be expressed was the essential physical apparatus of the older tragic hero. Alexander Rae failed vocally in the role of Ordonio (*Remorse*,

B.Strutt del.   Royce sculp

*—if ever you loved me & cherished me,
show it now, and tell while I have
breath to ask it:* ——————— *page 93.*

The frontispiece to Clara Reeve's novel *The Old English Baron* in which it is
evident that the stock types, here the old father, the male juvenile and the heroine,
were not the sole preserve of dramatists. (*George Speaight.*)

11

Samuel Taylor Coleridge, 1813) for, in spite of his expressive face and intellectual clarity, he suffered from an 'effeminacy of tone ... that [did] away with the impression of manly energy...'[34] Many popular light actresses took on the role of the younger heroine. When Mentevole (*Julia*, Robert Jephson, 1787), looking at a cameo of his sweetheart, rehearsed her virtues he was describing not one but a hundred heroines:

> O what a slender form is here! her polish'd front,
> Blue slender veins, winding their silken maze,
> Through flesh of living snow. Young Hebe's hue,
> Blushing ambrosial health. Her plenteous tresses,
> Luxuriant beauty! Those bewitching eyes,
> That shot their soft contagion to my soul ... (3.1).

The sameness of the heroine's role posed a problem for actresses, as Mrs Lister discovered while taking the part of Barbara in a revival of *The Iron Chest* (George Colman the Younger, 1796):

> ... [she] sung her airs in her old way, which is assuredly very pleasing, but her compass is so narrow that she may be said to have a *cuckoo* voice – hear her once, and you have heard all that she can do.[35]

The villain brought dynamism and vitality to the play. William Barrymore, in spite of his 'laboured enunciation' was judged by Thomas Dutton to be 'the best stage tyrant the theatre can boast'.[36] It would be possible to multiply instances of this type-casting but these few examples give an indication of the expectations the performer hoped to match.

The stock characters worked their way through repetitions of stock situations and devices. Strangely the audience seemed not to tire of these but found interest in the differing circumstances of each usage. Mention is made here of a few of the more common devices of the gothic stage. Mistaken identity was a convention which allowed a spate of horrors to be unleashed in the last act of the piece. The ending of Hannah Cowley's *Albina* (1779) was typical. With the darkness of night shrouding the characters, Edward mistook Editha for Albina and, whilst he embraced her, Gondibert, making the same misassumption, plunged his dagger into Editha's back. Rapidly avenging her death, Edward attempted to stab Gondibert who snatched the dagger from him and with it procured his own demise. The speed and complexity of the action, the gloom of the stage and the intensity of feeling produced a horrific but satisfying ending to the play.

Disguise was another theme which ran through many a gothic drama. It was a device which worked only within the framework of the stage, for characters were not permitted to question the identity of the disguised person, an accepted convention reliant on the eighteenth-century love of masquerading as a person other than oneself, whether at a masked ball or at the private theatricals which were so popular a feature of great houses or even at a fantasy such as the rituals Sir Francis Dashwood and his companions indulged in as the 'Monks of Medmenham', a village near Henley-on-Thames.[37] Disguise offered a character an extra dimension within which to operate. It also infused the situation within which the disguised person operated with overtones of irony, strengthening the link between the performer and his audience as a bond of complicity was formed between them. For example, the central character of *The Carmelite* (Richard Cumberland, 1784), Lord St Valori, disguised through much of the play as the friar of the title, was able to move outside the main action and comment on it: the plot then revolved around the awaited reunion of Lady St Valori with her husband. In the early scenes of the play clues were planted which hinted at the troubled past of the friar. St Valori's disclosure of his true self was incidental but most of the disclosures made by disguised characters were a flamboyance, bringing the play to a climactic ending. In *The House of Morville* (John Lake, 1812) Sir Thomas attended Hugh's trial masked and disguised; both were thrown off with electric effect at the the apex of the crisis. Rodmond the villain stood 'terror struck' and the presiding judge showed 'an expression of astonishment'. 'Oh, Heav'n' cried the prisoner, 'it is my father' (5.6). Here the device of the disclosure of identity was interwoven with another, the discovery of a long-lost relative.

The facility with which one recognised one's kindred, for 'relationship like murder, will out' (3.1), was parodied by Richard Sheridan in *The Critic* (1779): his strictures, however, did not inhibit the gothic dramatists. The speed with which recognition was achieved in *The Castle of Andalusia* was as rapid as in Sheridan's burlesque. With a rush the banditti, headed by Caesar their leader, entered the hall of Scipio's castle. From Scipio the briefest of questions – 'Where's now my son, Don Caesar?' – instantly elicited a revelation. Follies of the preceding years were washed away in a couple of sentences, lacking in intensity and pathos:

> Don Caesar: My father! (*Kneels to Don Scipio*).
> Don Scipio: How, my Son, Don Caesar!
> Don Caesar: Yes, sir: drove to desperation by –
> My follies were my own – but my vices –
> Don Scipio: Were the consequences of my rigour. –
> My child! Let these tears wash away the remembrance
> (3.4).

Little more than a frivolous explanation of the cause of the rift was given. Other causes·of the separation of relatives were varied, ranging from the prosaic to the fantastic – the Empress of Greece (*Valentine and Orson*) in flight from her husband gave birth to twins in a wood, one of whom was carried away by a bear. It was however rare for the cause itself to influence to any degree the structure of the plot.

As well as these situations, several stage properties were used with a measure of repetition and incidents were created around them; the principal properties were the intercepted letter and the phial of poison. Some letters were forgeries as lacking in credibility as the conventional disguise: 'Then this unravels all' (2.2) cried the Doge in *The Venetian Outlaw* (Robert William Elliston, 1805) on reading that Vivaldi had been falsely implicated in dealings with the banditti. Plans of escape could also be outlined in letters. The flight of Agnes (*Aurelio and Miranda*, James Boaden, 1798) from the convent was thwarted when Aurelio discovered a missive outlining the details. Similarly Bireno (*The Law of Lombardy*, Robert Jephson, 1797) gained written information of a plan to rescue the Princess of Lombardy which offered the recipient an opportunity to share his strategy with the audience:

> Confusion! Rescue her! Come back, Ascanio!
> Fly to St Mark's, collect the cohort there;
> Go, place them instantly around the prison!
> Bid them disarm the guard that holds that place;
> And, on their lives, drive back the populace (5.1).

In each of these plays the letters were more than conveyances of information; they instigated further action and became an integral part of the plot structure.

The phial of poison was a suspense mechanism. John Kerr used it to effect in his play *The Wandering Boys* (1814). Roland determined on the use of a slow poison for the two sons of the Count de Croissy which he would administer by inviting them to take some refreshment. The Count, disguised as a servant of Roland's, brought in various comestibles whilst keeping an eye on the bottle of poisoned wine that his master had introduced onto the table. Throughout the meal – lengthy for a stage repast – the audience was able to watch with growing suspense the Count adroitly switch the bottles and so poison Roland. The extraordinary length of time the drug took to become effective, for poison used as a means of resolving the action on stage usually worked with a degree of speed, was a cause of renewed suspense and it was not until two further scenes had passed that the Count opportunely told Roland, still not suffering from the effects of the draught, that it was he, not the boys who had been poisoned: 'He who composed the hellish drug best knows how long or short his time of lingering, or what may be his torments' (2.3). Audiences demanded finality from the poison. This was lacking in *The Inquisitor* (Thomas Holcroft, 1798) when the Patriarch, like a *deus ex machina*, descended to the dungeon in time to prevent the young lovers incarcerated there from taking poison. This inconclusive use was condemned in the epilogue:

> . . .if sad Melpomene must have rotation,
> Let her dagger be sharp, and her poison-bowl brimful,
> As Cowslip's, who brings Rusty-fusty one, creamful:
> Let Juliet quite stabb'd be, and Romeo quite poison'd;
> And let not, by signal of moon just horizon'd,
> A Patriarch pop in, 'tween the cup and the lip so,
> Nor the Hero and Heroine dally and sip so!

Recurrent devices such as these were a further means of recognising the gothic qualities of a play; they added to its atmosphere and occasionally became telling symbols, capable of arousing terror and pity in the audience.

So far we have looked at various motifs in the plays, the setting of the play within its time and place, and the stock characters and devices. Our purpose has been to discover the common ground on which the dramas were constructed. Before we can begin to answer the question 'What constitutes a gothic drama?' we must be aware of one important formative influence on the plays: the ideas of the German romantic playwrights Friedrich von Schiller and August von Kotzebue.[38] The remarks of reviewers of Charles Robert Maturin's play *Bertram* (1816) highlighted objections to the German school. The *British Review* attacked the tone of the play:

> Rotten principles and a bastard sort of sentiment, such, in short, as have been imported into this country from German moralists and poets, form the interest of this stormy and extravagant composition.[39]

The *Monthly Review* was more specific in its objections. The author was charged with sapping 'the foundation of moral principle by exciting undue compassion for worthless characters, or unjust admiration of fierce and unchristian qualities'.[40] A romantic presentation of low-life or roguery together with criticism of the ruling classes was to some a cause of outrage. John Larpent, the Lord Chamberlain's Reader of Plays refused to grant a licence for Joseph Holman's direct translation of Schiller's banditti drama *Die Räuber* in the belief that the text offered an immoral glorification of brigandage. Holman was left to recast the subject matter, converting the banditti into Knights Templars, and to reissue the piece as *The Red Cross Knights* (1799).[41] Spotting Germanic themes became a game for critics, – one played by the *Monthly Mirror* in reviewing Lewis's play *The Castle Spectre*:

> Mr Lewis's intimacy with German literature is strongly proclaimed ... the *dream of Osmond*, his *Atheism*, *Reginald's* sixteen years immurement, (derived, probably, from *The Robbers*) and the frequent appeals to Heaven, with a levity unusual to our stage, are all *German*.[42]

The dark side of human nature, its greed, lust and power, its attempts to over-reach, its suspected godlessness, when openly acknowledged by playwrights caused distress; more than that, its exemplification became a direct target for the Tory publication, the *Anti-Jacobin Review*.

It is difficult to define the nature of gothic drama. The gothic was not a movement in the sense that it was built on clearly formulated principles. Instead, it can be thought of as an artistic climate assimilated by practitioners of a range of the creative arts. Its early manifestations were seen in such fantasies as the gothic temple which closed the canal vista at Shotover Park outside Oxford and in the delightful circuit walk and mystery ponds William Kent designed at Rousham House near Bicester.[43] It found expression in the interior design of houses which were improved to contain a gothic library and chapel, as at Milton Manor in Oxfordshire.[44] The sad reflections of John Dyer on human mutability in 'Grongar Hill' were an early manifestation of the gothic spirit in words, later developed by novelists who, in the expansiveness of their romances, were able to draw out a multiplicity of dark themes. It was to the novel that Bertrand Evans in his own work on the text of the gothic dramas turned in attempting to formulate a definition:

> A Gothic play ... is one marked by features which have long served to identify a Gothic novel.[45]

There was a danger that the formulary would become imprisoned in its own cross-references. However, Evans went on to list some of the characteristics which have been considered in this chapter:

> These features include specialized settings, machinery, character types, themes, plots, and techniques selected and combined to serve a primary purpose of exploiting mystery, gloom and terror.

Why exploit 'mystery, gloom and terror'? Whilst evenings of mystery, and even of terror, may be acceptable in the theatre, we might now think that there is slight hope that evenings of gloom will draw large audiences. Eighteenth-century taste would deny that assertion. In 1763 James Macpherson published translations purporting to be of the Gaelic poet Ossian's work, which was immediately admired for its wild spirit. Professor Hugh Blair, lecturing on this newly discovered poet, selected that paraphernalia in his works which appealed to readers – the darkness, hoary mountains, solitary lakes, old forests.[46] These were, he said, 'ideas of a solemn and awful kind, and even bordering on the terrible'; the effect of the motifs was to raise the reader out of himself to the sublime; in some measure they recreated the effect that the actual phenomena exerted on travellers in their original experience. A fellow professor,

James Beattie, looking at objects more terrifying than those Blair contemplated – vast caverns, overhanging precipices and stormy seas – realised that even aesthetic horror could, in turn, lead beholders to the sublime.[47] It was in this spirit that the 'mystery, gloom and terror' of the gothic dramas were acceptable in the theatre.[48]

A succinct definition of the gothic drama, then, is difficult to devise. In this chapter, however, we have seen that it was a reflection of the dark and wild side of human nature, mirrored in an equally violent natural world or in architectural settings which, in their ruinous state, spoke of human mortality. Although the gothic stage represented the psyche of eighteenth-century man – his innermost fears and longings – the presentations were of plays set in an undefined and romantically conceived mediaeval past. The plays were subject to Germanic influences which queried the traditional eighteenth-century concepts of social hierarchy, sympathy and respectability. Finally, we have been aware that the playwright's expression of the gothic was not an isolated art form: it was expressed through the visual and plastic arts as well as in verse and prose. The gothic was a spirit, moving where it would. Although it was a dark spirit, it was capable of illuminating some of the submerged recesses of human personality.

Chapter Two: A World Untamed

The gothic dramatists chose a limited number of settings for their plays and of these such natural locations as mountains and remote landscapes, forests of vast dimension, the sea-coast during a storm and dangerous caverns appeared with a frequency beyond mere coincidence. What common experiences, we are prompted to ask, led to the frequent use of these setttings? Certainly the eighteenth-century passion for travel to remote areas of Britain and Europe led to an appreciation of the untamed qualities of nature.[1] More-over it was a passion in which both the wealthy aristocrat and the man of more limited means could indulge. Although a land-owner as prosperous as William Beckford could journey to Italy with his servants, artists, doctor and coach loads of impedimentia, the means would not be closed for writers and clerics to make lighter forays to the English Lakes. On returning home, the delights and terrors of the tour could be relived in the theatre where some of the kinds of location encountered were again seen, this time on the stage. Often the heightened emotional responses of dramatic characters to the settings in which they were discovered coincided with those of the erst-while traveller.

Were playwrights capitalising on the nostaglia of those who had toured in setting their dramas within the locations listed in the previous paragraph? If so, this assumption raises implications. It points to the common nature of the experience of travel in which there would be a remarkable similarity of response to natural phe-nomena. All travellers were moved, wrote Dr John Brown of Cam-bridge, by beauty, horror and immensity and this led to an apprehension of the sublime.[2] Here was a state which could be experienced anew through a variety of media, including that of the theatre. Are we to suppose then that a fraction of the audience in the Georgian playhouse – those who had engaged in travel – tended to impose their enthusiasm for certain exciting locations on the remaining members of the audience?

The suggestion of such an imposition is a contentious point. Examples offered by other media may be cited. Certainly the subjects of landscape painting were designed to appeal to the educated, for they contained classical allusions and an elaborate symbolic iconography. However, it was the rich, and thereby the educated, who purchased paintings. A more popular medium, the novel, could be purchased by a wider spectrum of people because of its comparative cheapness. Nevertheless, detailed plots, the emphasis on character rather than on situation, style, wit and allusion all suggest that the appeal again was to an educated minority. The theatre, although a popular medium, preserved an appeal to the educated classes in its choice of subject matter – frequently the dramatisation of romances – and in the implied emotional underpinning of the stage settings, although this limitation of settings must have confined the options of the playwright when tackling the plot to a restricted series of situations. Wild and remote locations were mentioned frequently in travel journals. Of his visit to the Swiss Alps, the Revd William Coxe noted a response which many in the following years were to corroborate:

> I frequently quit my party and either go on before or loiter behind that I may enjoy uninterrupted, and with a sort of melancholy pleasure, those sublime exhibitions of Nature in her most awful and tremendous forms.[3]

In its transference of this location to the stage, the last scene of Thomas Holcroft's play, *A Tale of Mystery* (1802), is typical of many:

> *The wild mountainous country of the Nant of Arpennaz; with pines and massy rocks. A rude wooden bridge is on a small height thrown from rock to rock; a rugged mill-stream a little in the background ... (2.3).*[4]

The effect on the spectator of this desolate countryside was intensified by a growing storm, and by the innovative use of a musical

commentary composed by Dr Thomas Busby. Its purpose throughout the play was to describe the frame of mind in which each
character found himself and to intensify the activity, 'imitating
at once both passion and action', wrote a correspondent in *The
Times*.[5] The scenery, the storm elements, the music and the labours
of the stage crew combined to move the audience to wonder and
excitement. Once the scene was established, Romaldi, the villain,
appeared *pursued as it were by the storm*, to the accompaniment
of his own musical theme. Responding to this picture of the villain
struggling against inimical nature, the *Monthly Mirror* correspondent wrote:

> The last scene in particular has a most striking effect; the trees are
> represented in actual motion from the storm which, with the accom-
> panying music, is well suited to Romaldi's state of mind, whose dreadful
> guilt has made him a fit object of both earthly and divine vengeance.[6]

Romaldi's opening soliloquy, punctuated throughout by storm
and music, was interrupted by the approach of the miller, Michelli,
an epitomisation of honest goodness. Instantly the orchestra
changed from *mournful music* to a *cheerful pastorale*. The characters
performed in the same adverse conditions but the music commented
on an intangible, the effect of innate virtue on adversity.

A further direction at the beginning of this particuar scene noted
that *a rude wooden bridge on a small height [was] thrown from
rock to rock*. During the last quarter of the eighteenth century
audiences had grown accustomed to this motif; it signified that
at that perilous junction the climax of the plot would be acted.[7]
This was a motif which William Dimond employed fourteen years
later in *The Broken Sword* (1816). Dick's Penny Edition described
the scene as it was customarily presented:

> *The valley of the torrent – a footbridge is cast across the head of the
> torrent to the summit of a perpendicular rock, on which the ruins of
> a chapel are perceptible, L.U.E. (2.3).*[8]

Rigolio, picked out by the lightning, engaged in combat with Myrtillo, the boy hero. He struck the torch from Myrtillo's hand and
hurled him headlong into the torrent. Myrtillo floated on the agitated waters until Esteven could rescue him. The precipices, the
ruins – the symbol of mutability – and the precarious bridge all

The precariousness of the bridge across the torrent and the danger for the traverser are romantically expressed in this watercolour by William Payne. (*Fitzwilliam Museum, Cambridge.*)

Scenes designed for toy theatres form a valuable record of the décor of many productions; here Hodgson records the conjunction of rocks and a somewhat solid water. (*George Speaight.*)

spoke of the vulnerability of man; but the constant rescues in the gothic drama told afresh of his strength of spirit gained by grace and virtue. Obviously so exciting a scene needed a realistic cascade and therein lay a difficulty. If a cyclical channel of water producing an unending cascade was used, the machinist had to be adept at getting the light to fall correctly or the gush of water was invisible from the auditorium.[9] A clumsy but sometimes more effective ploy was to use a tin cascade. Both of these methods had been mentioned by Garrick:

> When tin cascades, like falling waters gleam,
> Or through the canvas bursts the real stream . . .[10]

The representation of water was a difficulty with which not only the machinist wrestled. The Revd William Gilpin, whose indirect influence on stage design has not been recognised, wrote of the representation of waterfalls: 'Happy is the pencil, which can seize the varieties, and brilliancy of water under this circumstance'.[11]

The limpid quality of water made an effective contrast with the immutability of the mountains as George Colman the Younger was aware when he set the opening scene of his 'pantomime' *Feudal Times* on the edge of a lake surrounded by wild hill country.[12] Against the shoreline huddled a small village and from the centre of the lake rose Fitzalan's gothic castle. The scene-painter, Thomas Greenwood the Younger, and the machinist, Alexander Johnston, used the water to produce a note of light-heartedness:

> *A boat puts off from the Castle. All the men in the boat are dress'd in the Uniform of Baron Fitzalan ... The boat proceeds from the Castle, and at last reaches the shore of the Village. The boat and men appear small at first, and larger as they approach to keep up the perspective* (1.1).[13]

Either small children stood in as the diminished figures, dressed in costumes identical to those of their adult counterparts, or pasteboard figures and boats were used.[14] Johnston had worked on the same principle in organising approaching processions of elephants in Colman's *Blue-Beard* (1798), making the creatures from mechanical parts.[15] The idea of hiring real elephants from Pidcock's Menagerie in Exeter Exchange was abhorrent to him: 'Not I! if I cannot make a better elephant than at Exeter 'Change, I deserve to be hanged'.[16] As with the boats, small children were used to personate distant adults. Edmund Kean's first appearance on stage was as the diminutive figure of the tyrant Abomelique.[17] Colman made further capital from his lake setting by planning a return journey, accompanied by the songs of the villagers. They marched in procession to the boats, which disappeared behind a rock and then reappeared in diminished perspective. On arrival at the castle steps, 'men', the children of the company, disembarked. It was such moments as these made the piece, in Sally Siddons's words, 'the grand new spectacle.'[18]

In the composition of settings such as Colman's lakeside vista, there lay a parallel with the theories of the seeker of the picturesque, that traveller who stood at the prospect stations in the Lake District and composed idealised scenes in his Claude glass.[19] With his back

24

to the prospect he would open two hinged mirrors and, holding the small apparatus above his shoulder, move the reflection from one glass to another, slipping in a coloured filter if this enhanced the result, until he had created his picturesque composition. Such a man was Henry Tilney (*Northanger Abbey*) who spoke of 'foregrounds, distances and second distances; side screens and perspectives; lights and shades'.[20] William Gilpin, in describing his method of creating an idealised landscape, might have been writing about wings, borders and shutters at Drury Lane:

> A dark foreground makes, I think, a kind of pleasing gradation of tint from the eye to the removed parts of the landscape. It carries off the distance better than any other contrivance. By throwing the light on the foreground all this appears to my eye disagreeably inverted. – Besides, the *foreground* is commonly but a mere *appendage*. The middle, and remote distances, (which include the compass of the landscape) make the *scene*; and therefore require most distinction.[21]

An interjection at this point may be helpful for readers unfamiliar with the arrangement of the Georgian stage.[22] The proscenium arch created a division between the auditorium and the scenic area. Immediately behind this arch hung the green proscenium curtain which was raised at the beginning of the play and usually remained so until the drama ended. In front of the proscenium arch, jutting into the auditorium and flanked by stage boxes, was the proscenium or acting area. At the beginning of the period under survey actors tended to limit their performance to this flat apron, making their entrances by means of the proscenium doors on either side of the stage, set next to the arch. However, as the Georgian theatre became more sophisticated, the action moved up-stage, away from the audience, into the scenes area behind the proscenium arch.

Scenery consisted of double shutters which ran in grooves let into the floor of the stage, matched above by upper grooves. Required locations were depicted on these shutters which were manipulated into place by the stage-hands. When Drury Lane was rebuilt in 1794 seven sets of stage grooves, as well as trap doors, were provided; precise details of the earlier arrangements are not known.[23] Thus it became customary to draw aside shutters in a down-stage groove to reveal a scene, ready set, further up-stage.

These scene changes usually took place in full view of the audience. The shutters were framed by a series of wing pieces on either side of the stage, corresponding to the subject of the backscene.

In returning to Gilpin's description we see that his 'removed parts' have their parallel in the pictorial effect set up behind the frame of the proscenium arch, composed of the wings, borders above, and ground rows on the deck of the stage. On these were depicted the 'middle distance'. The 'remote distance' corresponded to the painted view on the backscene.

Gilpin wrote too of lighting. The stage was lit by Argands, an improved form of oil lamp. A row of these – the footlights – was let into the front of the stage and, by a primitive mechanism it could be lowered beneath the level of the stage, so producing a diminution of the light.[24] Further lamps were hung in clusters in the wings to illuminate the wing-pieces and backscene. An observation made as early as 1760 by Jean Georges Noverre is apposite in this context: '... the art lies in knowing how to distribute the lamps in uneven groups, so as to bring out the parts which require full lighting and to leave in shadow or darkness, as may be required, the other parts.'[25] Five years later the *Annual Register*, commenting on the increased number of lamps set up in the wings, remarked that 'the disposition of lights behind the scenes ... cast a reflection forwards exactly resembling sunshine'.[26] Gilpin mentioned the desirability of a dark foreground and one sees here a relationship with the proscenium in the theatre. W. J. Lawrence told the story of a member of the audience who flung a note to Junius Brutus Booth the Elder during one of his performances.[27] In order to decipher the writing Booth took it to the footlights. From this move Lawrence surmised that the proscenium lay in an area of gloom. However, another explanation is possible. English visitors to the Comedie Française had been surprised at the prevailing darkness on the proscenium of the French theatre; faces of the actors, when they neared the footlights, 'seem[ed] as if they were over Embers'.[28] The English forestage was obviously more brightly lit especially after the introduction of gas but one convention of the stage suggests that the light was patchy, allowing some areas of the proscenium to remain relatively dark. In both *The Iron Chest* and

Claude Lorraine, 'Hagar and the Angel'. (*National Gallery, London.*)

The Free Knights (Frederick Reynolds, 1810) an actor was directed to conceal himself upstage (2.2 and 2.1 respectively), suggesting that this was an area of darkness, whilst other characters downstage discussed private business. At the time of the latter play the whole area of the Covent Garden stage was lit by three hundred patent lamps: with that number available, any dark areas must have been intentionally created.[29] This is an aesthetic detail worth stressing, for the contrasts of light and shade gave an atmospheric quality to the performance of the gothic drama. Presumably Booth could have taken his note to a more brightly lit part of the stage as bring it to the footlights. The qualities Gilpin appreciated in a darkened foreground may be exemplified in Claude's landscape, 'Hagar and the Angel'.[30] In this, whilst much of the ground near to the frame is dark, the two principal characters are made evident by shafts of light. Claude's paintings illustrate the lighting effect machinists were to achieve ultimately.

In both the gothic romance and the gothic drama a recurrent setting was that of the forest with its special qualities of vastness and terror. To convey this impression of size on stage the playwright had to repeat the direction, *Another part of the Forest.* Gone were the kindly glades of Arden: ... *more entangled and intricate* (1.4) William Dimond noted of the forest in his play *The Foundling of the Forest* (1809). To intensify its fearsomeness he depicted it whilst a storm was raging:

> ... *The Tempest becomes more violent, and the stage appears alternately illumined by the lightning and in utter darkness.*

The stage forest, in common with the mountain landscape, established the physical insignificance of man. It was a place of transit through which the poor and the dispossessed made dangerous journeys. A cut wood, consisting of layers of fretted wing pieces which allowed further parts of the wood to be glimpsed, afforded an opportunity for Florian to make his entry through the scenes. His journey was eventful. As the storm raged a vivid lightning flash illumined the path before him, displaying *the figure of a masqued Bravo, Sanquino, with an unsheathed poignard advancing between the trees.* Obviously an accurate employment of the lightning was necessary but it is difficult to see how this was achieved. Occasion-

This scene of Webb's, designed for the toy theatre, gives a clear impression of the construction of a cut wood in which framing piece of scenery was mounted in front of a backdrop, useful for suggesting the vastness of the forest. (*George Speaight.*)

ally the machinists failed. The Countess of Bessborough complained of the storm in *Pizarro* in which the flashes of lightning were not 'properly tim'd' nor was the thunder 'well managed'.[31] An article in *All the Year Round*, written as late as 1872 but because of the conservatism of stage management acceptable as evidence, spoke humorously of the notion of 'storing lightning in a bottle', for in 1767 Joseph Priestley, in his book, *The History and Present State of Electricity*, had written of wires and Leyden jars.[32] In the theatre the more common means of simulating lightning was to ignite a small quantity of a compound of nitrate of barytes, sulphur, nitre, arsenic and charcoal, which burnt with a green flash.[33] The amount of activity seen by this suggests the light was not quickly extinguished as with an electrical flash but had a more sustained character. Adelmorn (*Adelmorn the Outlaw*, Matthew Gregory Lewis, 1801) remarked, 'Already, too, bright lightnings quiver along the glen' (1.2), implying that the lighting had a lingering, flickering quality. Philippe Jacques de Loutherbourg used a cut sky cloth behind which the lightning could travel.[34] Thunder was created in the theatre by shaking a thin sheet of copper suspended on a chain, as recommended by de Loutherbourg, a method replacing the earlier Georgian thunder run situated beyond the ceiling of the auditorium, and fitful gusts of wind were simulated by rubbing together two disks of tightly stretched silk.[35]

When Florian spied the Bravo, he struck his hand against a tree, the trunk of which was *hollowed by time, and open towards the audience*, remarked obviously, 'Ha! a tree!', and then hid within the aperture. Such functional trees were a feature in forest representations, their sturdy construction allowing performers to climb into the branches. A scene in *The House of Morville* began with the direction: *Hugo de Morville descends from a tree* (5.3). A similar type of tree was required in a scene set in the Forest of Orleans in *Valentine and Orson*. Considerable demands were made on it for not only did Valentine climb it, he used it as a lookout post and stripped its branches. In a chase the tree then had to support both Valentine and Orson:

> ...*while [Orson] is climbing up one side Valentine gets down on the other, and in turn beckons his opponent* (1.5).

Obviously sturdiness was an important factor.

In addition to the storms which raged through the forests, mists were needed to give the location a yet more fearsome atmosphere. de Loutherbourg had popularised a method of hanging a gauze between the spectator and part of the scene, using downstage wings and borders as a frame.[36] An adjustment of lighting then meant that only part of the area beyond the gauze could be seen: in gloomy patches people or objects could be hidden until suddenly revealed by illuminating them or by raising the gauze. Several layers, with an intervening space between each gauze, could given an impression that the forest really did stretch to that infinity suggested by the playwright.[37]

As a number of views of the forest were often required in a single play, it was necessary at times to use an appropriately painted drop-cloth. These served well as carpenters' scenes, allowing more elaborate settings to be marshalled behind them. Lit solely by the footlights, there was little opportunity for the terror suggested by the location to be made real. It therefore became an important task for the passing travellers to create the atmosphere of the location verbally. In *De Monfort* (Joanna Baillie, 1800) the central character, burdened with guilt, made his way along a *Wild Path in a Wood* (4.1), frequently listening for sounds of his pursuer. The screech-owl terrified him:

> Foul bird of night! what spirit guides thee here?
> Art thou instinctive drawn to scenes of horror?

However, once the terror of the forest had been established, a virtuous character could dismiss the fear as the imaginings of a guilty heart:

> Ha! does the night-bird greet me on my way?
> How much his hooting is in harmony
> With such a scene as this! I like it well.

In no scene was the human predicament more acute than in the representation of storms at sea. The helplessness of mankind in the face of catastrophe was magnified by the size of the waves and their sheer destructiveness as they drove ships onto a rocky coastline to disintegrate in flotsam. The subject found expression

Webb's sea-storm scene from *Union Jack*. (*George Speaight.*)

so frequently in painting that it developed its own characteristics
as a genre and the popularity of Turner's storm-ridden seascapes
may be calculated from the numbers of mezzotints that derived
from his compositions.[38] Shakespeare, in *Twelfth Night* and *The
Tempest*, had established the convention of opening the play with
a storm, at which point Charles Maturin placed the scene in his
drama *Bertram*. The tempest was viewed through a large gothic
window in the Convent of St Anselm. The audience was entertained
with the expected appurtenances of thunder, lightning, rain and
wind as information was conveyed by one of the brethen:

> A noble vessel, labouring with the storm,
> Hath struck upon the rocks beneath our walls;
> Her deck is crowded with despairing souls,
> And in the hollow pauses of the blast,
> We heard their perishing cries – (I.I).

A Drury Lane prompt-book notes that the fenestration of the room was set in the second grooves and that at the end of the scene the shutters parted to reveal tangible rocks over which monks clambered with torches, a scene 'sublimely grand and picturesque' reported the *Theatrical Inquisitor*.[39] In the background the exterior of the conventual buildings could be seen with their windows illuminated. Maturin, in juxtaposing the two scenes, had instinctively, for he was unused to writing for the stage, hit on a viable theatrical convention, the simultaneous comparison of situations involving peril and security. Instead of the musical accompaniment which Holcroft employed in *A Tale of Mystery*, Maturin created a collage of sound-effects as a background: there was the roar of the sea, signals of distress from a doomed ship, and the regular rhythm of the tolling of the monastery bell. An octagonal drum containing shells, peas and shot made wave-like sounds when revolved and the distress signals were suggested by hitting a large tambourine with a sponge fitted to a whalebone spring.[40] Several choices were given to the machinist when he represented the sea: in the earlier gothic dramas a series of parallel painted boards gave a stiffly undulating ocean; fully moulded wave rollers were also used. Later machinists favoured spreading a huge sea-cloth over the deck of the stage under which stage hands, lying on their backs, struck out vigorously with their arms and legs to create the waves, often a dusty process.[41] Which method was employed in *Bertram* is not known.

The last of the gothic landscape motifs to be considered is the cavern and here a contract may be made between its use in an early gothic play, *The Grecian Daughter* (Arthur Murphy, 1772), and that which featured so spectacularly in a later drama, *The Falls of Clyde* (George Soane, 1817).[42] In his play Murphy presented the exterior cavern to the audience. It was set to one side of a *wild romantic Scene, amidst overhanging rocks* (2.1). Possibly the cavern consisted of no more than a wing piece in which an aperture had been cut, leaving the other wings and the backscene to represent gnarled trees suggestive of the romanticism Murphy directed. The playwright gave only the briefest indication of a location, allowing details to be conveyed in the dialogue. Hence, in this scene it was left to Arcas to sketch in particularities:

In this section of an engraving by William Hogarth, 'Strolling Actresses in a Barn', 1738, moulded wooden wave rollers can be seen stacked against the wall. (*George Speaight.*)

Skelt's cavern set from *Aladdin.* (*George Speaight.*)

> . . . O'er the solemn scene such stillness reigns
> As 'twere a pause of nature; on the beach
> No murm'ring billow breaks, . . .
> A death-like silence through the wide expanse
> Broods o'er the heavy coast.

Even the time of day, some time before dawn had broken, was merely suggested in passing phrases: 'The stars in mid-career usurp the pole'. Within the cavern, guarded by Philotas, the aged and wrongfully deposed King of Syracuse Evander lay on the ground ill and sleepy. His daughter, Euphrasia, arrived at the scene to plead with Philotas for admittance into her father's prison. In neither action nor dialogue was there a suggestion that the character had scrambled over 'flinty rocks' to reach the desolate hideaway. One feels Murphy would regard such naturalism in the portrayal as an intrusive irrelevance. Eventually persuaded, Philotas allowed Euphrasia to pass into the cavern.

35

The following scene showed the *Inside of the Cavern* (2.2). It would appear convenient to place the first scene of the act well down-stage, perhaps in the second grooves, and to reveal the inner part of the cavern set in the third. A couch would then also be revealed on which Evander later rested. A doorway was placed in the backscene leading to an inner cavern in which the prisoner was detained. This was functional: Philotas opened it to display the king in his cell. The position of the couch in the scene seems to suggest that the performers, for at least part of the scene, played within the scenes areas and so identified more closely with the decor than was usual. The origin of the inner cavern was explained to David Garrick by Murphy: he had read an article in the *Spectator* describing a Syracusan cave known as 'The Ear of Dionysus', a place in which any sound was transmitted by a funnel to the ground above. Here political prisoners were kept so that the king's officials could overhear whispered secrets. However, Murphy did not incorporate any of these details into the stage directions.[43]

In 1813 the play was revived at Drury Lane. The prompt book for the revival suggested that, because the play had been a stand-by in the repertoire for over forty years, the convention of regarding the scenery merely as a hint of a location continued.[44] In the first of the two cavern scenes under discussion a set representing a 'Fisherman's Cave' was used. This was placed in the third groove. The cave opening in the scene allowed stock screens placed in the fourth groove to be seen. An indication of the time of day was roughly given by the position of the footlights, 'a little down', and by the note that the backscenes were lit by moonlight. At the scene change a setting referred to as 'Pizarro's Cavern' was positioned in front of the previous. A note in the prompt-book indicated that a 'large chain' was hung across the door leading to the cell. There was a warning note, too, that a couch was required, taken on, presumably, through the proscenium doors by the theatre's servants. If this was so, then the acting at this point had become disassociated from the scenery. The lamps continued to remain 'half down' but on the cue, 'The grey of morn breaks through . . .', they were raised to give greater light but without any special dawn effects. This revival of *The Grecian Daughter* seems to have been a plain production, making use of stock scenery

36

in which the decor played as little part as it had in the original presentation.[45]

When, however, we turn to the cavern scenes in *The Falls of Clyde* a different approach is evident. Here the scenes play an intrinsic part in the action:

> *An outer branch of the cavern; the entrance from without is through a narrow opening, high up in the rock. A brazen lamp is suspended from the arch by a chain; a ladder lies on the ground below, by the side of which is Ellen, as if just fallen. Donald is looking down from the opening. Ellen rises with difficulty* (2.3).

The drop between the high opening and the deck of the stage was an opportunity for action and excitement; the injured Ellen was chased by a band of gypsies up a ladder which reached to the aperture. Great excitement was aroused when Donald let himself down into the cave by means of a rope and then helped Ellen to escape by climbing to the opening, which he achieved in spite of an injured foot. Thus the scenery had become an important part of the action, and the actor no longer observed the distinction between the scenic area and the proscenium.

In presenting cavern scenes on stage, and many were used as locations, playwrights were expanding a theatrical setting which found its parallel in many an English garden, the grotto. To this place the landowner or his visitor could escape to indulge in the solitary emotion of melancholy. A splendid grotto was to be found at Stourhead in Wiltshire, a circular domed chamber from which the contemplative could look to the naturally lit cave of the River God where John Cheere's luminous blue statue stood. In his resemblance to Salvator Rosa's engraving of Tiber, the god gave evidence of the influence of the Neapolitan painter on the English gothic.[46] Occasionally, as at Pain's Hill, a grotto would become a hermit's residence, a place in which to install one of the estate's servants on visiting days.[47] Mrs Delany described the detailed care which Lord Orrery had taken in creating a miniature stage setting of the grotto-cell of an absent hermit on his estate near Dublin:

> ... the floor is paved with pebbles, there is a couch made with matting, and little wooden stools, a table with a manuscript on it, a pair of spectacles, a leathern bottle: and hung up in different parts, an hour-glass, a weatherglass, and several mathematical instruments, a shelf

of books, another of wooden platters and bowls, another of earthen ones, in short everything that you might imagine necessary for a recluse.[48]

Here is an instance in which the gothic theatre directly contributed to the design of a feature of the landscape; this grotto may be compared with Alvar's hermit cell in *Remorse* with its orderly collection of plants and the apparatus of the herbalist's craft.[49]

If the landscape scenes in this survey are compared with a number of Rosa's paintings, the extent to which playwrights were indebted to that artist is evident. He provided them not only with mountains, forests, crags, caverns and the weird grasping branches of stunted trees, but he also suggested to playwrights the way in which this landscape could be peopled.[50] Looking at his paintings, Sir Joshua Reynolds observed:

> Everything is of a piece: his rocks, trees, sky, even to his handling, have the same rude and wild character which animates his figures.[51]

The 'rude and wild' figures to be found on his canvases were the banditti, 'eminently suitable for scenes of wild grandeur', claimed William Gilpin, 'for they exhibit traits of greatness, wildness or ferocity', qualities in his estimation which touched on the sublime and could raise the spectator to those heights.[52] So it was that the banditti added terror to scenes in the gothic drama. Fear lay in the expectation that they lurked behind each projecting wing piece. Vivaldi (*The Italian Monk*) described the landscape created by the scene-painter at the beginning of the play:

> That arch between two rocks suspended, one
> Topp'd by the fortress-towers, the other crown'd
> By the tall pine and spreading oak, produces
> All that we claim for picture, saving only
> The human figure, to give life and action (1.1).

Then his imagination quickly supplied the missing people:

> Groups of banditti, ready to burst out
> On the unguarded traveller...

Sometimes the banditti were felt to be natural as well as social outcasts, 'a wen on order's face, that feeds on its own destruction'. Gondibert (*The Battle of Hexham*, George Colman the Younger,

Although outside the period of this work, Skelt's figures for James Robinson Planché's drama *The Brigand* show the traditional costumes of the banditti; to be noted are their cross-gartering and large flamboyant hats. (*George Speaight.*)

1787) gave a description of the bandit's life of isolation and tension that was at variance from the common romanticised presentation:

> Our perils, nightly watchings,
> Our fears, disquietudes; our jealousies,
> Even of ourselves? – which keep the lawless mind
> For ever on the stretch, and turn our sleep,
> To frightful slumbers; where imagination
> Discovers, to the dull and feverous sense,
> Mis-shapen forms, ghastly and horrible . . . (3.3).

Heroic characters might be forced by circumstance to become robbers: Lamott (*Fontainville Forest*, James Boaden, 1794) did so in order to support his wife and child and Count di Zulmio (*Edgar*, George Manners, 1806) hid amongst the bandits until it was expedient to reveal his presence. Honour would not debar a virtuous

39

person from becoming the leader of the banditti, as did Lindor (*The Sicilian Romance*, Henry Siddons, 1794) who was later constrained by the same virtue from betraying his charges.[53] It was these characters who added excitement and terror to the landscape and whom wary travellers feared as they journeyed through the circuitous plots of the gothic dramas.

This chapter has been concerned with the natural settings frequently used by gothic playwrights: mountains, precipices and torrents, lakes, forests and caverns. These were repeated so frequently in the theatre that they became conventional settings. But it was not in the theatre only that the settings appeared. Since the seventeenth century the subjects had captivated the painter's eye. Many a novelist had utilised such settings, too. The landscape designer had employed them, although the scale on which he worked was a diminution of the rugged, natural scene, and people walking through the great parks of England were delighted by the mound, the cascade, the wilderness, the lake and the grotto.[54] Here were 'scenes' in which the ambulant could perform as if in a play, simply by their presence in an appropriate setting. Furthermore they could appreciate the sentiments appropriate to these locations – the melancholy of the grotto or the terror of the water cascade – sentiments which were again engendered in the theatre, sentiments which, it has been suggested in several of the illustrations, originated in the natural wonders to which the Man of Sentiment had responded whilst engaged on the Grand Tour. We have observed in passing, too, that human figures seen against wild and tempestuous phenomena – monks struggling over the storm-washed rocks or banditti springing from their mountain lair – could, when viewed from a safe distance – the safety of one's box at the theatre, or the secure remove of the connoisseur viewing these figures in a landscape painting – lead the spectator towards an apprehension of the sublime.

As the period of the gothic drama progressed and its emotional spring wound up, so playwrights desired to heighten the impact of their work, to lead men to the sublime with a regularity that became self-defeating. This desire found expression in the gradual integration of the performer with his scenic background. As in paintings, man was conceived as a diminutive being, pitting the strength of his spirit against the untamed grandeur of a sublimely savage world, a far cry from the urban surroundings of Drury Lane and Covent Garden.

Similarly a desire for heightened responses led to the birth of melodrama – or, according to its root meaning, 'music drama' – in which a musical commentary not only intensified the impact of the action but also made an overt statement of the inner feelings of the characters in the play.[55] *A Tale of Mystery*, presented in 1802, was often instanced as the first of the melodramas, although there had been hints of this means of presentation eight years earlier in John Philip Kemble's play, *Lodoiska* (1794) which is looked at in the following chapter.[56]

These considerations are based on the suggestion that educated members of the audience called the tune in determining the content of the gothic drama. Playwrights made an appeal to their educational formation and their aesthetically developed sentiments. It is not possible to marshal a Euclidian type of proof for this proposition but we have seen pointers towards its probability. The gothic drama could be enjoyed on many levels; characters, situations, moral conflicts, all offered material for the consumption of the least sophisticated theatre-goer and it was this catholic appeal of the genre which suggests that educated taste opened the drama to a wide and appreciative audience rather than limiting it to a few *cognoscenti* retrospectively savouring the sentiments of their past travels.

Chapter Three: Castle and Cloister

As certain specific features of the landscape were recurrently portrayed in the gothic drama, so were two building types, the mediaeval castle and the conventual church. This is an understandable trait for, as Richard Payne Knight demonstrated, these two types were lasting models of 'pure Gothic' architecture.[1]

From the early years of the eighteenth century castles were viewed in a romanticised light, exemplified in the popular renaming of Claude Lorraine's painting 'Psyche outside the Palace of Cupid' (1664) as 'The Enchanted Castle', and reflected in John Keats' lines on the painting in which he described the palace as 'a Merlin's Hall, a dream'.[2] This remote view of the castle gave place to a more personal one as landowners built castles throughout the eighteenth century. The overall size mattered little. On a vast scale William Beckford commissioned John Wyatt to build Fonthill Abbey in Wiltshire, in no sense a monastic building, but an ostentatious monument in which its owner enacted the role of a cultured recluse.[3] Its purpose, as a scenic theatre in which one performed one's daily living, was the same as Walpole's Strawberry Hill, but on a vastly enlarged scale. Beckford lacked entirely Walpole's scholarly approach to detail, with his ceilings and fireplaces meticulously copied from fourteenth and fifteenth-century precursors.[4] Gothic enthusiasts visited these edifices. A schedule of open days and admission tickets had been formalised by Walpole.[5] Fonthill was less accessible than Twickenham and the visitor who traversed Wiltshire on his arrival found the front door opened by a dwarf in order to increase the sense of scale.[6] Spectacular effects were

A prosaic castle from Skelt's scenes for *The Woodman's Hut* but nevertheless this does suggest the multi-levels employed in such settings. (*George Speaight.*)

not lost on visitors. George Colman the Younger recorded his visit to Raby Castle in County Durham, a fourteenth-century shell within which its eighteenth-century owners constructed comfortable gothic apartments:

> As we passed through the outward gate of the Castle the vapour was dense upon the moat, and we were enveloped in night fog, while the rolling of the carriage wheels and the trampling of the horses hooves sounded dolefully over the drawbridge.[7]

He went on to imagine himself about to become a prisoner in this Bastille-like edifice, and it was not until the carriage rolled through double doors and he alighted before a fire in the warm entrance hall that his spirits rose. Sentiments such as those initially felt by Colman could only be developed fully within the leisurely pages of the gothic romance. The castles of Ann Radcliffe were

43

imbued with immensity, age and atmospherics. One has only to read a couple of sentences of *The Mysteries of Udolpho* to appreciate this:

> ...a part of the roof of the great hall had fallen in, and all the winds from the mountains rushed through it last winter, and whistled through the whole castle so, that there was no keeping one's self warm, be where one could. There, my wife and I used to sit shivering over a great fire in one corner of the little hall, ready to die with cold ...[8]

The compression of time required for a drama did not allow the full development of emotions of melancholy and terror. Furthermore, when castles were built on the stage, something of the small scale and obvious artifice of Strawberry Hill, which they resembled, robbed them of that mystery which Keats discovered in looking at Claude's mist-wraithed Palace of Cupid. The castle revealed in the first scene of *Richard Coeur-de-Lion* (Leonard MacNally, 1786) was prosaically domestic in its proximity to the tavern:

> ...*a strong Castle and its Environs, situate in a Wood.*
> *On one Side a Public-house, with the sign of the Harp* ... (I.I).

It was not until the stage castle was invaded by alien troops hauling scaling ladders over the walls and unfurling banners from the battlements that the canvas fortification became an integral part of the drama. Fires and explosions around the edifice could create an intense excitement in the watching audience. If the castle setting were to be fully exploited in this way, then a variety of backstage departments had to work together in harmony. The designer of the playwright's castle was the scenic artist but when fires and explosions occurred then the aid of the machinist was sought for not only did he arrange the pyrotechnics but he was also responsible for constructing towers which would disintegrate and a drawbridge capable of collapse. The involvement also of the acting-manager was essential, if his actors were to use the scenic and mechanical devices to the full.

Thomas Greenwood the Elder designed the scenes for John Burgoyne's version of *Richard Coeur-de-Lion* (1786). An engraving of the exterior of the castle in which Richard was imprisoned shows that the principal feature of the design was the variety of levels on which the action took place: these consisted of a raised terrace,

44

'Kemble *and* M.ʳˢ Jordan *in the* Characters *of* Richard & Matilda *in* Richard Cœur de Li
Act II. Scene 1.

Thomas Greenwood the Elder's castle set for John Burgoyne's *Richard Cœur-de-Lion*; to the left Dorothy Jordan as Matilda and on the right John Philip Kemble as Richard. (*Theatre Collection, University of Bristol.*)

a moat, trucks on either side of the stage supporting fortifications spanned by a drawbridge and to stage left a high tower topped by a parapet.[9] Here was scope for exciting spectacle and if this scene, described as *the inner works of an old fortification* (2.2), was basically the same design as the final scene of the play, the *Castle assaulted by Matilda's troops* (3.2), an impression of the activity on the set is gained from Burgoyne's directions:

> *Blondel and Sir Owen encouraging [the troops] ... the garrison received a reinforcement, and repels the attack with advantage ... Blondel then puts himself at the head of the pioneers, and leads them to the attack ... the assault continues ... Richard appears on the Fortress without arms, endeavouring to free himself from three armed Soldiers ...*

There is presumably a degree of verisimilitude in the directions as General Burgoyne was a key commander in the American War.

Excitement was added to the sight of fighting soldiers by the fall of one of the towers. Collapsing buildings consisted of patches

45

of constructed scenery which were extracted from the main erection and hauled out of sight by the stage-hands; backstage workers, too, pulled supports from beneath sections of towers causing a sudden descent.[10] Hinged sections which fell to pieces by a tug on a rope were also used. Percy Fitzgerald writing in the second half of the nineteenth century criticised such mechanics: 'We can distinctly see the broken portions working smoothly on a hinge'.[11] The critical faculties of the audience were, however, distracted by concurrent explosions and flashes created by stage-hands dropping lycopodium, a flammable powder derived from dried moss, onto braziers strategically placed in the wings.[12] Accompanying the activity was *a loud and animating flourish on all the instruments* followed by the playing of a march. Layers of action and sound were intensified by the beseigers unfurling Matilda's colours, bringing an added texture to the scene. The play drew to a conclusion as Matilda ran across the upper level of the fortress into Richard's arms, a silent mime eloquently telling of happy endings. This convention of adding layered elements was obviously effective and became an established practice, used still in musicals. The final tableau into which the cast, singing a chorus, formed was a visible signal of the restoration of order.

John Philip Kemble's play, *Lodoiska* was the first of the gothic dramas to be staged in Henry Holland's new Drury Lane. The plot concerned two lovers, Florenski (Michael Kelly) and Lodoiska (Anna Maria Crouch) and their rescue by Kera Khan, the Tartar chief, from Ostropol Castle where they had been imprisoned. Three settings, unusually few for a gothic play, were employed, and the printed text credited the painters of each: the first scene, the exterior of a moated castle in the Forest of Ostropol, was by Thomas Greenwood the Elder; Thomas Malton, Thomas Lupino and J. Demaria painted Lodoiska's tower apartment; and Greenwood was responsible for the final scene, a hall and gallery in the castle, aided by Rudolf Cabanel, who had designed the stage area and its machines and who masterminded the conflagration at the end of the play. Although the scenes were judged to be magnificent, long delays between changes held the performance up until after midnight.[13] Possibly the staff were unused to the elaborate machinery installed in the new building. Cabanel had provided for wings,

A quaintly articulated Castle of Ostropol designed by Thomas Greenwood the
Elder for John Philip Kemble's musical romance, *Lodoiska*. (*Theatre Museum;
by courtesy of the Board of Trustees of the Victoria and Albert Museum.*)

ground rows and backscenes to be moved upwards from the cellars
through sloats whilst further pieces could be lowered simulta-
neously from the fly-gallery, all of which should have made for
speedier transformations. During the second change one of the
carpenters mangled his hands which accounted for some of the
delay.[14]

As before, it was the final scene which riveted attention. Hodgson's sheets of toy theatre characters give an indication of its
appearance: a conventional gothic hall was built with two large
mullioned windows at the rear; through them the Round Tower,
and behind that a further turret, could be seen; a terrace provided
staging for much of the action outside the hall.[15] Midway through
the scene *the doors of the Hall are burst open ... and a crowd of
Tartars rush in* (3.1). The open doors and the windows would allow
the fighting and fires outside the Hall to be seen, neatly framed,

while the unperforated section of the back-scene would screen such stage machinery as braziers, each containing a bellows, burning flares and reflectors of silk moreen which cast a red glow on the stage.[16] As in the previous play the final incidents were performed without dialogue:

> *An engagement commences between the Polanders and the Tartars; the Tartars having stormed the Castle, which they Fire in various places, the battlements and towers fall in the midst of loud explosions. Lapauski and Lodoiska are discover'd in a blazing tower; Floreski rushes through the flames and rescues them.*

Darting flames, up to eighteen feet in height, appeared as stage-hands pumped the bellows.[17] Possibly, too, extras disguised as Tartars would run across the stage refuelling the braziers by throwing further quantities of powder on them. Music played an essential part throughout the drama. Harking back to its role, and comparing it with Holcroft's use of music in *A Tale of Mystery*, a writer in the *Monthly Mirror* noted that 'language, situations and passions' were accompanied and heightened.[18] The correspondent went on to give an instance. As Kera Khan attacked Lovinski's castle to rescue Lodoiska, the tyrannous baron armed himself for the assault, interjecting his preparations with brief questions and commands. A 'martial symphony', played between each of Lovinski's short speeches, added to the audience's impression of the agitation of the Baron's mind. This accompaniment, claimed the writer, 'had the most pleasing effect'.

Needless to say, the spectacle of this scene was a risk to the performers. They suffered from the intense heat of the flames and the choking smell made speaking difficult, a possible reason for eliminating the dialogue. One evening a draught fanned flames towards Mrs Crouch as she appeared amongst the upper masonry. Although she felt a scorching, she remained at her post for fear the effect should be spoilt. Michael Kelly realised the danger she was in:

> I ran up the bridge which was a great height from the ground, towards the tower, in order to rescue her; just as I was quitting the platform a carpenter prematurely took out one of its supports; down I fell and at the same moment the fiery tower, in which was Mrs Crouch, sank down in a blaze with a violent crash; she uttered a scream of terror.

Providentially I was not hurt by the fall and, catching her in my arms, scarcely knowing what I was doing, I carried her to the front of the stage, a considerable distance from the place where we fell.[19]

The heroine related to her biographer the audience's reaction to so near a catastrophe:

...the loud plaudits which [Kelly and Crouch] received from the audience, who thought their acting uncommonly excellent, roused them from their apprehensions for each other, and at the same time convinced them of the *effect*; which they found was far superior to any studied scene, as their danger and their fears happened to be well-timed and perfectly in character...[20]

These dangers pointed up the necessity for a close co-operation between the various theatre departments. Gone were the days when the machinist merely provided an isolated special effect. Spectacle, a feature of Holland's theatre, demanded harmony and singleness of purpose amongst the design staff, as well as the careful rehearsal of the actors on the finished set.

George Colman fully utilised Drury Lane's potential for spectacle in his production of *Feudal Times*. The plot was based on an oft-repeated formula: the heroine, Claribel, had been abducted by the villain, Baron Ruthenwolf, and imprisoned in his castle; Edward Fitzallen, young and heroic, needs must go to rescue her. Inevitably Ruthenwolf's castle was surrounded by Fitzallen's troops in preparation for the final battle. Glimpses of various corners of the castle were afforded by this plot, including the quaintly named Banquet Gallery, a mediaeval 'Colonade' and the castle ramparts over which the final skirmishes were fought. Colman's elaborate description of the last scene reflects the set which Greenwood the Younger designed for him:

On the right of the stage is the exterior of Ruthenwolf Castle. The chief entrance is represented in a side view; consisting of a Gateway, between two Turrets; – the Bridge drawn up. The Castle is partially moated; the water losing itself under a low arch, beneath the battlements, before it has compleatly encircled the building; ... Above [the battlements], a black round Tower.

From a window in the round Tower, ... are flights of steps, which communicate with the ramparts. On the left of the stage are high tufted trees:

49

At the back, Mountains, in perspective, and the Sun rising above them
(2.5).

The concluding spectacle consisted of the disintegration of the
Round Tower, Ruthenwolf's charge, Matilda's escape by boat, a
second explosion and the collapse of a turret, the death by drowning
of the villain and the anticipated final tableau representing the
triumph of true love accompanied by a chorus sung by soldiers
and vassals. A writer in the *Monthly Mirror* found the play a 'dull
but showy drama'; he did, however, commend Greenwood's
scenery, Johnston's mechanics and Miss Rein's costumes as examples of the 'Sublime and Beautiful'.[21] Colman had utilised the standard tricks of spectacle which in this case worked and even James
Boaden, jaded by repeated theatrical explosions, recognised that
they had their uses:

> On the subject of this eternal stage practice, let me say to the credit
> of their sappers and miners that it invariably succeeds ... A blow-up
> at the end of the piece was formerly a metaphor and signified its per-
> dition; it is now a reality and ensures its success.[22]

Colman was vague about the period in which the play was set,
offering only passing references to wars between the barons. Greenwood, therefore, approximated to styles and concentrated on the
physical spaces required by the action. A regular correspondent
to the *Gentleman's Magazine*, who signed himself 'An Antiquary',
yearned for an accurate representation of historical buildings and
costumes on the stage. He found much to displease him in *Feudal
Times*: the appellation 'Banquet Gallery' drew his fire, the 'Colonade' was 'in a mode of architecture entirely new', the dome above
it inappropriate for 'antient structures' and the castle itself was
'too undetermined to mark any of our antient styles'.[23] These
remarks highlight changes in the expectations of the audience. Previous easy acceptances of an approximation to the mediaeval had
been summarised by Walpole: 'Old castles, old pictures, old his-
tories and the babble of old people make one live back into centuries
that cannot disappoint one'.[24] Walpole conjured up visions, in
Herbert Butterfield's phrase, of 'a mediaeval world that could never
have had any existence' but towards the end of the eighteenth century the architecture of the mediaeval world was brought into focus

by the scholarly surveys of the Society of Antiquaries.[25] Other works, such as Richard Gough's *Sepulchral Monuments* (1786–99) and John Carter's *Ancient Monuments of England* (1795–1814) sharpened the visual perception of the audience. Greenwood's castle designs had become out-moded.

An atmosphere of moral gloom was prevalent in the gothic castle. It was in the villain's nature to make that gloom palpable; he sucked the light from the castle apartments.[26] From its owner the castle took its character. 'This house is melancholy's chosen home,' said Count de Valmont (*The Foundling of the Forest*) describing his castle in the upper regions of Alsace, 'and its devoted master's heart, like a night bird that abhors the animating sun, has been so long familiarized to misery, it sickens and recoils at the approach of mirth' (1.2). Similarly Motley's exclamation in *The Castle Spectre* that Conway Castle was 'the most melancholy mansion' (1.1) was immediately followed by a description of the dark scowl and louring eyes of Earl Osmond who stalked through its halls and vaults. A degree of over-statement was necessary in the appearance and behaviour of the villain if he was to epitomise the darkness and evil present in his domain. This, combined with his dynamism, made him a figure of sublime terror.[27]

The incarcerating power of the castle was only fully appreciated when its subterranean passages and dungeons were presented on the stage and the audience, viewing these locations, must have experienced a tension for it was faced with a dichotomy: emergent Romanticism stressed the liberty of the human spirit but at the same time the idea of the constriction of one's freedom held a fascination.[28] In reality working people, and some professionals, were keenly aware of the constant threat of imprisonment for debt and of the workhouse in old age.[29] Travel made foreign prisons objects of curiosity. John Montagu, for example, on his tour of Sicily in 1738 had been intrigued by the overgrown quarry-prisons of Syracuse and by the 'Ear of Dionysus', later used by Arthur Murphy in *The Grecian Daughter*.[30] Highly imaginative and theatrical designs for prison buildings were created by Giovanni Piranesi in his work *Carceri d'Invenzione* in which the authority of those responsible for the inmates was symbolised in the weight of arch soaring above arch.[31] Horace Walpole remarked on the scale of these sombre caprices: 'He piles palaces on bridges and temples on palaces, and scales Heaven with mountains of edifices'.[32] These engravings, popular in England, graphically expressed the morbid interest playwrights, scenic artists and audiences were to discover in the subject.

Matthew Gregory Lewis was no stranger to the subject of incarceration, exploiting to the full the theatrical elements inherent in the situation. The dungeon which figured prominently in the final act of *The Castle Spectre* passed into theatre lore and was parodied in such plays as *The Rovers* (George Canning, John Hookham Frere, George Ellis, 1799). Two dungeons appeared for good measure in Lewis's play *Adelmorn the Outlaw*, both in the third act. An idea of the first dungeon may be gained from the description given by the 'Antiquary':

> A Dungeon, consisting of a Saxon recess, with plain collumns [*sic*], and an extensive flat arch, which arch, to suit the purposes of a vision, rises to an enormous semi-circular opening, where are seen rocks, mountings, fires and ghosts. The management of this half-terrific and half-ludicrous spectacle is not without its share of merit, as far as the mechanist is concerned.[33]

Within this dungeon Adelmorn, the hero of the piece, was discovered in chains. Lewis's stage directions give an impression of the above mentioned vision mimed to a chorus sung by 'Invisible Spirits':

> *Part of the wall opens, and discovers (in vision) a blasted heath by moonlight. The figure of an Old Man, a wound on his bosom, and his garments stained with gore, is seen holding a bloody dagger towards Heaven* (3.1).

As thunder rumbled, the moon turned red and Ulric, the villain, appeared held by two demons. In retribution the Old Man plunged the dagger into Ulric's breast. Overtopping this pantomime a 'Glory' appeared towards which the Old Man ascended on clouds! Only a brief carpenters' scene intervened between this and the following dungeon setting, a tour-de-force for the machinist: in its course the walls of the place of confinement were struck by lightning and an inner cell was discovered in which had been immured one of Lewis's long-term prisoners, Father Cyprian, seen against flashes of lightning visible through a broken gothic window. On the first

The sheer weight of William Turner's prison interior is suggestive of its punitive value to the traditional guardians of order. (*The Turner Collection, the Tate Gallery, London.*)

night Lewis's hapless dialogue had amused the audience at the start of the scene but later on derision greeted the disintegration which the 'Antiquary' claimed was 'devoid either of mechanical skill or picturesque effect'.[34]

The most original of Lewis's dungeon settings appeared in *Venoni* (1808) staged at Drury Lane. It was a double scene, described in his memoirs as a 'novelty on the English stage'; the directions indicated the layout:

> *The scene represents the interior of two ... vaulted Dungeons ... They are separated by a Wall of immense thickness, supposed to be that which divides the Monastery of Saint Mark from the Ursuline convent. The Dungeon to the left of the Audience contains a miserable pallet ... the other dungeon is entirely dark; in the back is a large iron-grated door, through which a winding Staircase afterwards becomes visible. – On each side of the door is a kind of Tomb formed of rough-hewn Stone* (3.1).[35]

The Times added a few extra details and an interesting gloss on the 'removal of the fourth Wall' technique of presentation:

> The side next the audience of both of these dungeons is represented to be removed to that the audience sees at the same time what *Josepha* is about in the convent dungeon, and what *Venoni* is doing in that of the monastery ... these dungeons do not come quite to the front of the stage and are raised upon platforms so that they look like two dens for wild beasts, an appearance to which certain spikes placed to prevent their contents from leaping on the stage, very much contribute.[36]

The lighting directed the attention of the audience to Josepha (Sarah Siddons) in her location at the beginning of the act, and the audience accepted this convention; it was when Venoni (Robert William Elliston) was flung into the other dungeon, which by that time was illuminated, that the audience found the dual setting disturbing. Venoni's discovery of a weakness in the dividing wall and his consequent success in dislodging some of the stones (Lewis's memoirs suggest he hurled lumps of mortar into Josepha's cell!) drew the full disapprobation of the spectators. Apparently the pair resembled figures in a weather house, and members of the audience could not understand why Elliston should not leap over the spiked front to the next cell. A puzzling feature of the description in *The Times* is the suggestion that the setting should be brought in front

54

of the curtain line onto the proscenium. Possibly the setting, in order to avoid overspill from the auditorium lights, was placed well upstage of the proscenium arch, thus unfortunately impairing audibility. Mrs Lewis complained to her son that she was unable to hear Josepha.[37] However, it is difficult to determine the exact positioning. The unfavourable reception drove Lewis to rewrite the third act of the play immediately; but until the revision was ready for performance the management temporary brought the partition 'to the front'.[38] Again, the exact placing is hard to picture: was 'the front' the curtain line? or was the setting in part on trucks and shunted downstage onto the proscenium? Furthermore, we might ask how the new position was acceptable to the audience. In his rewrite of the third act Lewis deemed it prudent to show a single dungeon, the home of Lodovico for the past twenty years, into which Venoni was flung and from which, with considerable speed, he escaped.[39]

It is salutary to compare Lewis's dungeon scenes with one from a play by Sophia Lee, *Almeyda, Queen of Granada* (1796). The setting was a Moorish castle built on a rock overhanging the River Guadalquivir. The stage direction was promising enough:

> *A dark vault irregularly hewn in the rock, extending out of sight on one side, in a vista of rude imperfect pillars. A small gate leads on the other side, through an enormous crag of the rock* (4.1).

Within this setting Alonzo, the hero of the piece, was discovered chained to a rock, an effective opening tableau. The audience, and of course the scene designer too, had already been prepared for the setting:

> ... this steep rock
> Through many a winding path is coop'd in dens,
> Unknown – unpenetrable – one o'erhangs,
> An arm, which parting from the Guadalquiver,
> Deep-plunging seeks an undiscover'd course.
> There through a fearful chasm wild nature wrought,
> Full many a victim to the fears of state,
> Has sunk into oblivion (3.2).

However, the static quality of the dungeon scene failed to exploit the location. This lack of theatrical drive was a common fault

Pollock's scene for Isaac Pocock's *The Maid and the Magpie*, showing the prison setting complete with alcove within which the prisoner was chained. (*George Speaight.*)

of inexperienced gothic playwrights. From the outset Lewis had successfully guarded against such a criticism.

As the castle gained its character from that of the villain, so the dungeon became a more terrifying place through the presence there of a mysterious figure, the long-term prisoner. As early as 1748 Laurence Sterne expressed the Englishman's horror at the idea of life-imprisonment when he peered through a grated doorway at the wasted body of an anonymous wretch: 'thirty years ... he had seen no sun, no moon . . . nor had the voice of friend or kinsman breathed through his lattice . . .'[40] On stage two types of prisoner appeared. One was an aged man such as the Baron of Glendore (*Edgar*) who had been immured in the dungeon of his own castle for the previous twenty years. The other was the wronged wife of the villain kept prisoner within the castle that was rightfully hers; this is 'The Lady' of *The Sicilian Romance* imprisoned in a cavern deep within the rocks beneath the Castle of Otranto. These figures gave a fearsome reality to the dank prisons of the Georgian stage. Both of the plays mentioned were adaptations of novels by Ann Radcliffe thus giving an opportunity for readers to resavour in the theatre dark sentiments they had enjoyed when first encountering the characters.[41]

Occasionally a dissenting voice was raised against this unhealthy interest. Burlesque is a powerful weapon and the gothic captive was only one of a number of targets at which the authors of *The Rovers* aimed their barbed darts. In the description of the dungeon beneath the Abbey of Quedlinburgh it was plainly the dungeons of Lewis which were parodied:

> *Scene changes to a subterranean Vault ... with Coffins, 'Scutcheons, Death's Heads and Cross-bones. Toads and other loathsome Reptiles are seen traversing the obscurer parts of the Stage* (1.2).

Rogero, the prisoner of eleven years standing, appeared in a suit of rusty armour and in a lengthy soliloquy recapitulated on his sufferings and degradation. Recalling the inappropriateness of Lewis's Reginald (*The Castle Spectre*) breaking into song, the authors had Rogero accompany himself on a guitar to the tune 'Lanterna Magica', reminiscing on his long-past youth. Overcome, he banged his head on the dungeon wall and collapsed with a *visible contusion* as the scene ended.

When the gothic castle was translated to the Orient its nature changed. There was little to fear from the external appearance. But within, strange devices of terror seized the imagination. Greenwood the Younger, assisted by William Chalmers, designed the scenes for George Colman's oriental pantomime, *Blue-Beard*.[42] Here the castle of the monstrous Blue-Beard, Abomelique, was the focus of interest. A drawing of the exterior appears on the cover of Michael Kelly's musical score showing the construction as a frolic – some arabesque of fragile balconies and quaint Islamic minarets, a gothic pavilion suitable for a seaside resort. Was that the reason the *Monthly Mirror* found the castle 'offensive to the eye of taste'?[43] The castle consisted of a buttressed rotunda from which stemmed an arcade with a covered walkway above; a substan-

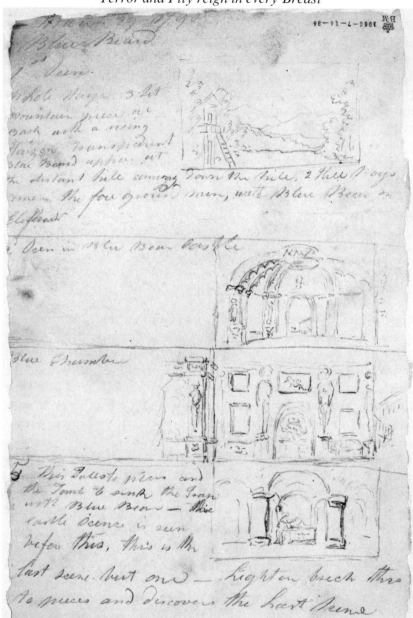

Drawings and notes on the sets for *Blue-Beard* made on the reverse of a water-colour by John Henderson Grieve; the scene in the Blue Chamber was eagerly anticipated because of its many mechanical devices. (*By courtesy of the Trustees of the British Museum.*)

tial tower stood to the fore, topped by a minaret. At the base of the tower the figure of Fatima, the heroine, serves as an indicator of the height of the construction: assuming she is five feet tall, then the height of the tower measured approximately eighteen feet. The rotunda, possibly not required to support performers, was slightly taller. In view of the height of the proscenium opening at Drury Lane, thirty-eight feet, the castle must have appeared as a bijou folly on stage, in spite of the expenditure of £2000 on the production.[44]

The real interest of this castle lay within. Provincial theatre managers made much of the horrors of the Blue Chamber on their playbills: Thomas Trotter advised that his Brighton audience would be terrified by the 'awful supernatural appearance of Blue-Beard's Murdered Wives, Spirits, Phantoms, and the Figure of Death, displaying the fatal Effects of Curiosity'.[45] Those fortunate enough to see the Drury Lane production were confronted with an apartment of wonders which made the castles of the northern gothic lands appear to be insipid cobwebbed erections:

Shacbac puts the Key into the Lock; the door instantly sinks with a tremendous crash and the Blue Chamber appears ... The interior apartment ... exhibits various Tombs, in a sepulchral building; – in the midst of which ghastly and supernatural forms are seen; – some in motion, some fix'd – In the centre is a large Skeleton seated on a tomb, (with a Dart in his hand) and over his head, in characters of Blood is written: THE PUNISHMENT OF CURIOSITY (1.3).

Later in the play the skeleton rose with the dart poised ready to plunge into the hearts of the unwary as the walls collapsed revealing a distant prospect of the country. The complications of these scenic marvels which Johnston devised got the better of the backstage staff on the first night, delaying curtain-fall until after midnight.[46] The articulated skeleton, too, posed problems. Michael Kelly, as well as composing the musical score, played the part of Selim, the hero, who at the end of the play vanquished the skeleton:

Where Blue Beard sinks under the stage, a skeleton rises, which, when seen by the audience, was to sink down again; but not one inch would the said skeleton move. I, who had just been killing Blue Beard, totally forgetting where I was, ran up with my drawn sabre, and pummelled the poor skeleton's head with all my might, vociferating, until he disap-

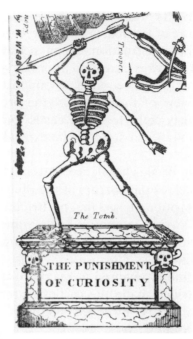

The articulated skeleton from Webb's Characters in *Blue-Beard*. (*George Speaight.*)

peared, loud enough to be heard by the whole house, 'D – n you! d – n! why don't you go down?'[47]

Three years after the first season, when Kemble revived the pantomime, Grimaldi was in the cast. It was his custom to make miniature models of noteworthy examples of stage machinery; one of these was the skeleton in *Blue-Beard*. He had perfected the workings of Johnston's design.[48]

The second of Payne Knight's models of 'pure gothic' mentioned at the beginning of this chapter was the conventual building. It had obvious links with the castle in as much as many of its inmates were regarded by playwrights as immured and subject to devastating punishments: 'You are to receive three hundred lashes on the back' (2.5), the Prior in *The Sicilian Romance* told Martin the sup-

posed novice. Often the conventual building was portrayed as a
place of intrigue and within its walls, especially in Lewis's plays,
ran a strong element of unregenerate lust. In England there were
few signs of the religious life to act as models for playwrights.
Several communities of monks and nuns expelled from France during the Revolution lived in remote domestic houses in Lancashire
and Dorset.[49] The life was private and unspectacular to the extent
that, when travelling outside their houses, the religious wore lay
clothes. What was known of the lives of monks and nuns was
brought back from Europe by travellers. Richard Colt Hoare
visited the Cistercian monastery at Casamare prior to the French
Revolution and found it occupied by 'men condemned to perpetual
silence, devoted to fasting and prayer, cut off from the society
of parents and friends ... and consigned to cheerless labour and
increasing mortification'.[50] It was, he thought, a place of extreme
penance and daily punishment. After the Napoleonic Wars Samuel
Rogers travelled to Rome where he witnessed a profession ceremony at a convent. In recording the experience he stressed his
horror at the irreversible withdrawal from society. One day a young
woman was at the opera, and the next she had passed through
the convent grille to the sound of the bell and the 'Miserere'.[51]
For both travellers contact with religious houses had been an
emotionally disturbing experience.

From 1794 William Capon was senior designer at Drury Lane.
As an enthusiast for mediaeval architecture, he brought to his work
a scholarly desire to represent on stage buildings with historical
accuracy.[52] He was responsible for the gothic convent chapel which
featured in Joanna Baillie's play *De Monfort*, one of his most spectacular constructions. Thomas Campbell described the setting as
'representing a church of the fourteenth century, with its nave,
choir and side aisles, magnificently decorated, and consisting of
seven planes in succession'.[53] The vista, fifty-two feet in depth,
receded to the back of the scenic area, using all of the available
sets of grooves. It was made the more mysterious by Baillie's direction that the setting was *almost dark* (4.2). Some of the conventional
gothic motifs played on the setting: a stormy wind beat on the
windows of the church and in the distance, by the light of torches,
a newly dug grave could be discerned. Theatrical capital could

61

be made from processions of monks or nuns, and the formality of these Baillie used to a purpose:

> *Enter a Procession of Nuns, with the Abbess, bearing Torches. After compassing the Grave twice, and remaining there some Time, whilst the Organ plays a Grand Dirge, they advance to the Front of the Stage.*

The orderly funeral hymn, sung by the nuns, was interrupted by a lay-sister, wildly disturbed, breaking into the tableau. Her entry was followed by the sound of hammering on the door and the announcement of a new catastrophe: 'I saw a murder'd corse stretched on its back'. The interruption of the solemnity was calculated to cause a temporary sense of outrage in the audience which, aided by the heavy splendour of Capon's church setting, together with 'procession, decoration and music' felt itself to be taking part in a religious ritual. Joanna Baillie, whose experience of the drama was confined to writing plays for the closet, instinctively created a theatrical situation symbolising the disorder which raged in De Monfort's breast and which, Macbeth-like, he spread amongst those with whom he came in contact.[54] Kemble's direction of the play ensured that ceremonial in the chapel should be effectively spectacular. He himself had been a seminarian at Douai Abbey in France and had experienced at first-hand some of the memorable externals of the religious life. Furthermore, as acting manager of Drury Lane, he took a pride in drilling the processions so that they became faultless, a concern for professionalism which met with occasional criticism from his actors.[55]

Performances of *De Montfort* received a mixed reception, but Capon's church setting was universally acclaimed.[56] 'The interior perspective of the convent,' wrote Thomas Dutton, '...ranks among the grandest scenes the stage can boast.'[57]

The setting had an interesting stage history for Capon experimented beforehand with a less ambitious chapel and after the production of *De Monfort* the church was adapted for several further gothic plays. In 1798 Capon painted scenes for *Aurelio and Miranda*, a dramatisation by James Boaden of Lewis's novel *The Monk*. The opening setting of Milan Cathedral, 'a fine specimen' may have served as a maquette for the *De Monfort* church.[58] Lewis's original novel had met with a shocked reception but Boaden's play

was a white-washed adaptation. Nevertheless, some disapprobation
fell on Capon's work and claims were made that 'it was sacriligious
to represent a church upon the stage'.[59]Such criticism did not inhibit
Capon. The setting was reused for a performance of *Julian and
Agnes* (William Sotheby, 1801) when it became the hall of a monastery in the Alps; the 'Antiquary' noted that it was hardly fitting
to use a 'sumptuously copied' setting of Westminster Hall for the
common room of 'a poor monastery on Mount Saint Bernard'.[60]
In May of the same year it was again spotted by the 'Antiquary',
this time in *Adelmorn the Outlaw*, 'cut up into parcels' serving
as a gothic hall in Count Ulric's castle, in spite of Sheridan's pro-
mise that new scenes had been created especially for the romance:

> How . . . can our minds reconcile side ailes, compartmented spaces under
> the windows, clustered columns, groined cieling [*sic*], etc., etc., in this
> place, as they are the characteristics of structures raised for devotion.[61]

Sheridan's financial mismanagement drove Capon from Drury
Lane in 1802 but his set continued to be adapted. That year at
the Passiontide oratorios the orchestra and singers were backed
by the westernmost section of the set, described in the *Gentleman's
Magazine* as 'the interior of an abbey' and 'a cathedral with every
appropriate decoration'.[62]

The disintegration wrought by time was a fruitful area for playwrights to explore using for their metaphor the ruins of castles
and convents. Painters used the motif to emphasise the fleeting
impermanence of life. Turner's watercolour of the remains of Llanthony Abbey, with its shades of pale blue and grey, reflected the
melancholy inherent in the ruin.[63] On stage this melancholy found
expression not only in architectural relics but also in the lot of
those who took shelter within them. Madam Lamotte and her servant Peter (*Fontainville Forest*) serve as an example of the dispossessed finding a temporary home in a decrepit abbey. The
playwright's interest in ruins was a reflection of the mid-century
habit of constructing one's own crumbling tower, artificially aged,
to serve as an eye-catcher, an enthusiasm which eventually led
to the appreciation of genuine remnants of mediaeval buildings.
A prebendary of York Minster wrote of the joy of possessing within
one's own grounds this genuine link with times past:

> ... happier far
> Ah! then most happy, if thy vale below
> Wash, with the crystal coolness of its rills
> Some mould'ring abbey's ivy vested walls.[64]

A like response had prompted Thomas Duncombe to construct a terrace above Rievaulx, along which visitors to his Yorkshire estate might wander, looking 'through a waving break in the shrubby wood,' wrote Arthur Young, 'which grows on the edge of a precipice, down immediately upon a large ruined abbey, in the midst ... of a small but beautiful valley'.[65] William Pearce used the situation of the landowner, wishing to 'improve' the view from his house by dispossessing his impoverished neighbour and destroying her cottage, in his operetta *Netley Abbey* (1794), an interesting social comment on the gothic movement. As the title implied, Oakland, the owner of an estate, was anxious to secure an uninterrupted view of a Cistercian abbey standing on the edge of Southampton Water: 'All to the westward must immediately be cleared; and by the fall of the leaf, I hope not a tree will be left standing' (1.1). In addition to removing the trees and Woodbine Cottage, Oakland determined to build his folly, a ruined tower, to complete the vista. The final scene, set in the ruins, gave scope for the painter, John Inigo Richards, to provide, in Pearce's words, 'the most Picturesque Portrait of a Gothic Ruin that the hand of Science ever produced'.[66] London audiences may not have been aware that the operetta was an ironic comment on a Southampton builder who bought the site, not to 'improve' it but to pull the abbey down. A fall of masonry killed him before he achieved damage other than to himself.[67]

The frequency with which the gothic castle and the conventual church appeared on the Georgian stage confirmed the appropriateness of Payne Knight's exemplification of these buildings as the models of the mediaeval world. When they were presented in a ruinous condition, their sentimental appeal was heightened. Possibly, in an age in which capitalism, industrialisation and scientific reasoning were burgeoning, ecclesiastical ruins suggested a passing of the old ways, the erosion of the mystical and transcendental elements of traditional Christianity. In their decrepitude both castle and convent were a symbol of human mutability: nothing of the permanent character of the inert mass of the mountain range and the contrasting dynamism of the cascading torrent was to be found in these remnants of human endeavour. As overpowering natural phenomena had sparked off a sentimental response, so crumbling remains provoked a sadness, a mourning for the vanished past, and a melancholy arising from the knowledge that fleeting hours ran parallel with encroaching decay. The gothic stage did not permit a positive statement about either of these building types. Little of the eighteenth-century love of 'personal improvement' was reflected in its plays; there was no portrayal of the institution, such as was happening in France, of new religious orders to alleviate ignorance or suffering; instead castles existed to be razed and convents to moulder.

The illustrations given in the chapter highlight the growing regard in the late eighteenth and nineteenth-century theatre for realism. From the audience's disapproval of the multi-locational setting of *Venoni*, we see that its members had strongly advocated a representational approach. Managers, for their part, were eager to respond. For instance, in portraying natural phenomena they tended to substitute real water for the canvas wave and the tin cascade and in presenting stage buildings complicated perspective-layered interiors gave an illusion of size and solidity, more so, in fact, than the box set, the end result of the quest for architectural realism, was later to do.

Scholarship aided the progress of the realist movement with its publications relating to historic costume, customs and architecture; but realism, of course, whilst it made use of this type of scholarship as a prop, was not dependent on it. Instead, experimentation with scenic construction and materials and advances in the use of lighting brought the 'real world' onto the confines of the stage. As we shall see in the next chapter, the introduction of gas lighting in the theatre was a temporary set-back for the realist approach for its harsh, overall light not only flattened the appearance of the stage but removed from it any sense of mystery. The technique of stage lighting had to be relearnt in the nineteenth century. Realism was advanced, however, through the growing practice of uniting the actor with his setting. Stage architecture encouraged this: the castle was a construction prepared for rampage by fighting

militia and its interior provided secret panels, windows, galleries, and furnishings, all of which the actor utilised and so became at home in the changing function of the scenic area.

These two chapters on the decor of the gothic play clearly show that this form of drama was integrated with the then current advances in presentation adopted by the managers of Drury Lane and Covent Garden. The retrospective gaze of its subject matter in no way deflected it from a lively and spectacular presentation. A microcosm of the work of the theatre at large was to be seen in the staging of the gothic play.

Michael Rooker's watercolour of Netley Abbey on the edge of Southampton Water. (*Sheffield Art Galleries.*)

Chapter Four: The Stage Spectacle

Throughout those years in which the gothic drama was popular the attitude of the London acting managers toward stage scenery changed. In the three decades from 1750 the scenes gave merely a rough indication of the locality of the action. *The Countess of Salisbury* or *Douglas* could be performed on a bare proscenium without any lessening of the audience's enjoyment for there was no interaction between the performers and the scenes. Hall Hartson, in *The Countess of Salisbury* (1764), made no reference in the dialogue to the locations within which his characters were placed, whilst John Home in *Douglas* (1757) sketched in the locations verbally only insofar as the circumstances of the play required. Lady Randolph, in her opening lines, highlighted the geographical details by which she was surrounded, hinting at their gothic nature:

> Ye woods and wilds, whose melancholy gloom
> Accords with my soul's sadness, and draws forth
> The voice of sorrow from my bursting heart,
> Farewel a while: I will not leave you long;
> For in your shades I deem some spirit dwells,
> Who from the chiding stream or groaning oak,
> Still hears and answers to Matilda's moan (1.1).

By the 1780's, however, playwrights incorporated their chosen settings within the drama. We have already seen that the stage castle developed from a two-dimensional depiction on the back-scene to a structure over which companies of soldiers could set up ropes and ladders to scale the wood and canvas walls. In Frederick

69

Reynolds's unpublished play, *The Crusade* (1790), platforms of various heights were set in position in front of scenes and wings from which the battery of the walls of Jerusalem took place.[1] Galleries and flights of stairs became a means of advance or escape in gothic halls and cavernous dungeons. Action gained an impetus from structural scenery.

One realises the importance of the scenery within the play when the setting alone drew the attention of the audience. The first minutes of Thomas Dibdin's pantomime, *Valentine and Orson*, staged at Covent Garden in 1811, consisted of a gradual day-break over Orleans. Then gates were thrown open and the King of France, victorious over the Saracens, triumphantly entered amongst his forces. The sunrise, splendid though it was, had been but a metaphoric expression of the royal approach. Although details no longer exist of the lighting arrangements for this entertainment something of its effect can be gained from W. H. Pyne's description of dawn breaking over London, as created by de Loutherbourg in his miniature theatre, the Eidophusikon, in Panton Street, off Leicester Square.[2] A faint light appeared on the horizon tinging the sky grey; saffron gave way to fleecy clouds as mists dispersed and then, the stage brightened by degrees, the sun appeared catching the gilding on the vanes and cupulas of the city. If these special effects in a miniature theatre do in fact reflect its larger and more elaborate counterpart, then it becomes obvious that such a spectacle depended on the close co-operation of the scenic designer and of the machinist responsible for the lighting. At Covent Garden the person responsible for co-ordinating this variety of skills was Charles Farley who not only stage-managed many of the spectacles but also directed the choreography and appeared as dancer, acrobat and actor.

Costumes were an important element in the visual presentation and these, too, were in the course of time co-ordinated by the acting manager. Two attitudes towards costume design are discernible. There was a desire for historical accuracy, contrasted with an attempt by the actor to gain a costume suitable for performance. The 'Antiquary' who found faults with the scenes in Colman's play, *Feudal Times*, was offended, too, by the costumes in the production. Realising that the author had omitted to give a precise date to the action, the 'Antiquary' described the costumes as 'those fancy stage-habits that we have been familiarized to witness on rustic stage characters for several years past'.[3] Soldiers appeared in armour pertinent to the time of Edward III, with corresponding shields but one commander wore a 'Roman habit'; a second appeared in a Grecian helmet, Caroline suit of armour, Jacobean ruff and a 'pair of common high topped gloves, such as we see worn by some old people' and a third was equipped with his own trumpet which he sounded from time to time. Little excuse could be offered for the discrepancies, for a parallel to the architectural publications of the Society of Antiquaries were reference works ranging from Thomas Jeffery's early volume *A Collection of the Dresses of Different Nations* (1757–1772) to Charles Hamilton Smith's later work, *Ancient Costumes of Great Britain and Ireland* (1814). A consultation of such books would not circumscribe the costumier's inventiveness. On the contrary; for James Planché, writing in 1834, noted that in attending to accuracy in stage dress 'a new spring of information and a fresh source of effect' could be discovered.[4]

The regard of the 'Antiquary' for accuracy was a far cry from the prevailing practice in the early days of the gothic drama. John Henderson serves as an example. In 1778 he began working at Drury Lane where the wardrobe was copiously stocked, providing all of the players with an outfit for each role and obviating the need to use one's own clothes and yet Henderson was content to wear the same coat for ten consecutive roles.[5] Fearing that the actor might appear unsuitably dressed for the role of Raymond in Robert Jephson's dramatisation of *The Castle of Otranto*, under the title *The Count of Narbonne* (1781), Walpole lent Henderson a costume from his own collection of antiquities at Strawberry Hill.[6] Under Kemble's supervision the holdings of costumes increased at the Lane and those made for given productions, due to Kemble's own antiquarian interests, were fashioned with a regard for accuracy.

However, actors felt that suitability for performance was as important as accuracy, and a simplification of stage costumes occurred in the early days of the nineteenth century. Percy Fitzgerald advocated that an indication of the period of the costume was all that was required, as long as the wearer considered the character portrayed and the action he engaged in.[7] Sarah Siddons had agreed with this approximation and eventually she ensured that her dresses were workmanlike.[8] Her costumes for the role of Euphrasia in *The Grecian Daughter* illustrate this simplification process. In 1792 William Hamilton painted the actress in a heavy, boldly patterned satin dress hung with weighty tassels.[9] This was not a practical garment for a heroine who clambered over rocks in deserted places, sought for her father in dark caverns and finally stabbed a tyrant-villain. Ten years later Mary Hamilton depicted Siddons in the same role in a much simpler classical costume, consisting of a plain tunic and coat.[10] This process of simplification allowed young performers to develop more sprightly personations, veering away from the statuesque playing of the Kembles, towards the dynamism of Kean and his followers.

The most direct way of making a spectacular impact was to mass numbers of costumed actors in a procession and it was this which Kemble made popular at Drury Lane, to the extent that a complainant in the *Theatrical Inquisitor* grumbled that audiences had 'no ear but for music, no eye but for processions'.[11] Richard Cumberland's sympathy for Kemble, who he imagined to be struggling 'against a torrent of mummery and machinery and song and spectacle', was wasted, for Kemble not only enjoyed the processions which featured in his productions, he also rehearsed them thoroughly.[12] Processions had become so firmly established at Drury Lane by 1822 that Robert William Elliston, by then the manager, employed Samuel Beazley to construct wing space for their assemblage.[13]

The several examples of processions given here are but a few amongst many. Only one scene in Frederick Reynolds's spectacular travelogue, *The Exile* (1808), was singled out for mention on a Covent Garden playbill: 'In Act II. The Coronation of the Empress Elizabeth'.[14] A front scene showed the exterior of the Cathedral at Moscow. Through a triumphal arch supernumeraries representing bandsmen, soldiers, knights, banner-bearers, heralds, clergy and Tartars made their way, until the climax was reached, the appearance of the chariot of the Empress drawn by six horses. Once the host had passed across the front of the stage, it regrouped

out of sight. The front shutters parted bringing into view a tableau
of the assembly surrounding the enthroned Empress over whom
the Patriarch held the imperial crown. George Daniel's edition
of the play, based on the prompt-copy, listed two pages of supernumeraries used in the ceremonial, an expensive entourage.[15] The
coronation of George IV prompted the management to revive the
play and the procession on stage gave Londoners the opportunity
to see a fictional replica of the English coronation procession.[16]

Death, with its symbols of yew trees, tombs, urns and skulls
was consonant with the gothic temperament, so it was to be
expected that death on the stage would be weighed down with
gothic trappings, Playwrights focused on the funeral as an opportunity not only for religious ceremonial but also as a point at which
to create tension in the plot. That in *Manuel* (1817) is an example.
Its author, Charles Maturin, a parochial clergyman, officiated at
many a plain Irish funeral but he nevertheless encrusted the funeral
of Alonzo with excesses. Before its entry the procession was
described:

> It is the warlike band that serv'd Alonzo:
> In sad and solemn march they onward come:
> His broken spear and helm are on a bier;
> Round it Spain's noblest warriors, dark and sad,
> With trailing lance and low-hung banner, tread
> To the near fane . . . (3.3).

In part this served as a stage direction. As the coffin came into
sight the orchestra played martial music. Manuel gripped the hand
of de Zelos whom he suspected of murdering Alonzo and, pressing
it to the centrally placed coffin, he attempted to force de Zelos
to declare his complicity in the death. de Zelos swooned, an
unmanly form of escape from a confrontation, more suited to the
gothic heroine's aversion of a crisis.

Presentiments of mortality were engendered by the procession
surrounding a prisoner's slow march to the scaffold, a metaphor
of life passing. Often the playwright worked against time: would
the promised pardon arrive before the execution took place? would
the innocent be claimed by death? In *The Law of Lombardy* Robert
Jephson staged a judiciary procession within the shadow of the

73

SCENE in the NEW TRAGEDY of the
Law of Lombardy
Mᵣ HENDERSON Mᵣ SMITH and MISS YOUNG in the Characters of
BIRENO, PALADORE, and the PRINCESS. See London Mag. for Feb. 1779

(*left*) Sarah Siddons in the role of Euphrasia in *The Grecian Daughter*, engraving by J. Caldwell after the painting by William Hamilton. (*Theatre Museum; by courtesy of the Board of Trustees of the Victoria and Albert Museum.*)

(*right*) The final scene from *The Law of Lombardy*. Paladore avenges the honour of the Princess against the calumnies of Bireno. (*Royal Opera House Archives.*)

gallows, emphasising the imminence of death.[17] 'Let the procession pass' (5.3), rang through the ranks as soldiers, senators, heralds and the condemned prisoner, none other than the Princess of Lombardy, made their way onto the stage to complete the tableau. The formal speech of the princess, from which the audience fully perceived the pathos of the situation, was interrupted by the cry of a messenger:

> Arrest your sentence!
> I come in the name of one who hears with horror
> This barbarous process, to proclaim the accuser
> Of that most innocent and royal lady,
> A slanderer and villain.

74

The stage picture, emphasising the harshness of the legal sentence, formed a contrast with the fragility of the heroine, a point which prompted the audience to feelings of pity. But the sudden breaking of the tableau by the messenger's hurried entry and the resultant informality caused by the excitement of the crowd served to sever the suspense that Jephson had created in his writing.

It is difficult to account for the popularity of processions in the gothic drama. Apart from the solitary link with the procession surrounding the thanksgiving for the temporary respite of George III's madness in 1789 and with the coronation procession of George IV, they reflected nothing of life outside the theatre, nor did they advance the plots of dramas, indeed they usually retarded the pace of the play. Some capital could be made when the procession served as a *memento mori*, a reminder of the falling sands of time and of the inevitability of death. There was, too, a metaphysical concept in which the procession represented a state of order, which could suddenly be thrown into confusion by the arrival of a representative of chaos.

Spectacular settings, elaborate costumes and the colourful effect of massed gatherings added zest to the gothic drama. There is another convention which obviously should be preserved of this genre – the representation of the supernatural on the stage – but Georgian audiences were doubtful about the propriety of the appearance of spectres.[18] Matthew Gregory Lewis introduced ghosts into a number of his plays and each was heavily criticised. This rejection was at odds with the importance devoted to the supernatural in other media. Henry Fuseli's paintings of supernatural beings were acclaimed and gothic romances such as *The Castle of Otranto* which allowed the paranormal full rein were popular; indeed Horace Walpole prophesied that Clara Reeve's novel *The Old English Baron* would be rejected for its rationalisation of seemingly supernatural events.[19] In contrast, the Anglicanism of the latter part of the eighteenth century was devoid of mystery, replacing the mediaeval necrophilic symbols of cadavers and skulls with emotionally uncharged Georgian funerary urns and broken pillars. On the defensive, playwrights made humorous depictions of appparitions. Requiring a ghost in *Fortune's Frolic* (1799), John Till Allingham utilised the prankster of the piece,

75

Rattle, dressing him as a spectre. It was tame stuff and lent little atmosphere to the play.

This scepticism is reflected in two contrasting plays. In the first, *Raymond and Agnes* (1809), Lewis took a legend he had incorporated into his novel, *The Monk*, and reworked it for the stage, presenting the audience with the Ghost of the Bleeding Nun. The second, by Coleridge, *Remorse*, in the tradition of the revenge drama in which ghosts had played an intrinsic role, showed Coleridge wrestling with acceptable ways to bring the 'murdered man' in a confrontation with the villain. In Lewis's play, Agnes had been immured in Lindenburg Castle and, with Raymond's help, contrived her escape by disguising herself as the Ghost of the Bleeding Nun. This led to confusion when the Ghost herself made several appearances. West's sheet of toy theatre characters shows the spectre clad in a blue habit with a white scapular and veil.[20] On the scapular a red cross was boldly emblazoned as well as the inevitable dashes of blood. There was little excitement in the spectre's early appearances, although at the end of the play the rear of a cavern fell to pieces as she was manifested in a *blue aethereal flame* (2.7). One of her disappearances occurred in a wood in which there was a mound for the ghost to climb and then vanish, presumably through a trap beneath. The effect was heightened as, according to Dick's edition of the play, a gauze hung between the audience and the spectre, allowing her plea for Agnes's protection, written on a scroll, to be rear-projected.[21] This intervening gauze was a stage mechanism with which Kemble had experimented previously when presenting Boaden's play, *Fontainville Forest*, in an attempt to gain a blue-grey haze.[22] The effect was partly achieved by using the green halves of the shades of the Argand lamps, strategically banking them in the wings.[23] Lewis's play was presented for several seasons in Norwich but it is significant that the supernatural subject matter hindered its presentation at the London patent theatres. However, Charles Farley's ballet based on the legend was presented to some acclaim at Covent Garden in 1798 and the seriousness of Farley's intention in staging this received approving comment from the theatre historian Walley Oulton.[24] A dual standard appears to have operated: ballet, with its acceptance of fantasy, was able to accommodate material which the

Theodore.—" HOLY ST. MICHAEL, PRESERVE ME.*"—Act 2, scene 3.*

A scene from *Raymond and Agnes*, an 'interesting drama' by Matthew Gregory Lewis, as depicted in Dicks' Penny Plays. Theodore is terrified by Agnes disguised as the Ghost of the Bleeding Nun. (*George Speaight.*)

legitimate theatre found unacceptable.

Lewis was undeterred by forewarnings against using spectres in his plays; Coleridge's attitude was one of caution. In *Remorse* he wished Ordonio to be confronted by the ghost of Alvar, his supposedly murdered victim. Although this was a device which Jacobean writers used in presenting the disintegration of the villain in such tragedies as *The Changeling*, by 1813 supernatural apparitions were so disfavoured that Coleridge was forced to employ an alternative: Don Alvar, not in fact murdered but living in disguise as a wizard, was helped by his friends to stage before Ordonio a conjuration in which a picture of the attempt on Alvar's life became illuminated. Coleridge strove to gain an atmosphere of mystery: the setting, the Hall of Armoury, was designed by William

77

Capon who had joined forces with Greenwood on the production; from the start of the conjuration scene soft music was played on an *Instrument of Glass or Steel* (3.1) and mysterious voices sang invocations to the soul of Alvar; incense rose from the altar, clouding the area where the illumination would occur; ascending flames hid the illumination once its message had been received.[25] Many of these devices had heralded the apparition in Friedrich von Schiller's drama *Der Geisterseher* (*The Ghost Seer*) and Coleridge may have had them in mind. Wisely the audience was allowed no time to reflect on the credibility of the scene; immediately after the illumination the *familiars of the inquisition* burst through the doors of the hall and dragged the perpetrator of this 'most foul sorcery' to the dungeon. When the play was staged it was not the apparition scene, as Coleridge had feared, which found disfavour, but the protracted poetic diction.[26] Thereafter the supernatural was transmuted to the region of magic and brought out only in pantomime.

Ghosts were not a formula for success in the development of spectacle in the gothic dramas. An alternative had to be found. In 1811 John Philip Kemble was searching for a sure money-spinner for Covent Garden to which he had transferred from the acting management of Drury Lane. The expedient he adopted was to revive Colman's pantomime, *Blue-Beard*, inserting two interludes in which riders and horses were to feature. Selim and the Saphis galloped on stage prepared to attack Blue-Beard's castle. The effect of the sudden entrance of these twenty animals and riders from Astley's Amphitheatre was electrifying as, with drawn swords, the cohort appeared to be about to attack the pit and yet, at the same time, the effect could be touching.[27] The Countess of Bessborough cried silently as Fatima, standing on the castle tower, waved her handkerchief singing of her expected release.[28] A hint of the sturdiness of the set is gained from the stage direction: *They gallop off over bridge and practical hill at rear* (2.1). In the second interlude the horses appeared on the castle battlements. A collapsing drawbridge and a leap by a trio of the equine performers over the moat provided further excitement. William Hazlitt noted that the horses generated the real dynamism, for when fights ensued the riders wielding swords resembled 'the impassioned images that tap the

The cover of the music to *Blue-Beard* showing Fatima sighting the Saphis about to attack Blue-Beard's castle. (*By permission of the British Library E*109/*TP;* 79/30579.)

hour on Saint Dunstan's'.[29] Little pity was felt for human casualties. A black steed, John Williams reported, 'threw his incumbent over the bridge, with as much dexterity and as little feeling as a qui-tam Attorney'.[30] The pathos of a dying horse won the affection of James Boaden; the wounded animal, hearing a pistol shot, 'sprang suddenly upon his feet as if again to join or enjoy the battle, but his ardour, not being seconded by strength, he fell again as if totally exhausted'.[31] In these falls, declared an American visitor, the horses died 'as gracefully . . . as the English tragedians'.[32] Hazlitt remarked on the final scene of carnage:

> The other horses, by this time, are disposed also in their respective attitudes; the dismounted warriors are seen fighting across their bodies; drums, trumpets, smoke, and confusion complete the effect; and the close of the scene lets loose a thousand exclamations in praise of the new performers.[33]

Cartoon lampooning John Philip Kemble's use of animals in lavish spectacles at the Theatre Royal Covent Garden; these tended to displace productions of Shakespeare. (*Royal Opera House Archives.*)

A spirit of curiosity prompted the first-night audience to attend, but its gratification was instant. Toy theatre sheets give a visual impression of the performers. Webb's and Bailey's plates show the figures in Abomelique's entourage, foot soldiers, oriental musicians, camels bearing gifts, child attendants and Fatima in a sedan.[34] Whilst actors braved elephants and horses, the camels remained unmounted. Probably the smell of the livestock ('the stench was so abominable,' wrote John Genest) within the confines of the stage deflected performers from riding on the odoriferous beasts.[35]

When the revival of *Blue-Beard* reached its successful zenith, Lewis was asked by the Covent Garden management to provide

RON AND THE **ELEPHANT.**

an afterpiece in which the new equine craze might again find vent. He wrote *Timour the Tartar* (1811) with its self-contained interludes for horse and rider. One of the highlights of the play was Agib's rescue of his mother, Princess Zorilda, and it is interesting to compare the reports of two spectators with the original description in the text:

> *([Agib] seizes a banner, leaps his Horse over the Parapet, and disappears. The Georgians give a shout of admiration, and all rush towards the Water).*
>
> *Oglon*: ... She rises ... She struggles! He's near her – he extends the banner ... She has missed it! ... Huzza! She has it! She grasps it! and See, See, See! her arms are around the neck of her Son!
>
> *(The Horse rises out of the water, bearing Agib and Zorilda)* (2.3).

81

Some of the characters in Lewis's hippodrama *Timour the Tartar* from Skelt's toy theatre sheets. (*George Speaight.*)

The Times correspondent was obviously captivated by the bravado of the spectacle and the skill of the animals:

> [Zorilda] ... springs from a height which really appears too perilous to give pleasure to the spectators. She is seen struggling in the waves of the cataract, and her child plunges in on horseback to save her. After rising from wave to wave, the Princess and her son gain the land and ascend the cascade on horseback. They are received at the summit with shouts of joy by the Georgians and the Castle is attacked.[36]

Crabb Robinson, more reserved in his enthusiasm, committed his impression to the pages of his diary:

> *Timour the Tartar*, I am ashamed to say, kept me awake after I had been drowsy during the play ... on one occasion the heroine having leapt from a height and being buried to appearances in a stream – her son appears on horseback (a boy Master Champion) rushes into the water, disappears and returns with his Mother behind him on the horse. Though apparently among friends the boy then gallops with his Mother behind him *up* the cataract!!![37]

Covent Garden enjoyed many revivals of *Timour* for the play contained those elements which have been explored in this work: there were the exotic scenes set in a distant land, the colourful effects of massed costumes, the well-drilled processions and tableaux under Farley's direction and the marvels of the steeds. However, there were complaints against the hippodramas. Lord William Pitt Lennox, himself a keen equestrian, regretted that they displaced the comedies of Garrick, Foote and O'Keeffe.[38] In May 1811 pittites were showered with anti-hippodrama leaflets as they themselves waved placards.[39] Provincial actors complained vociferously of the injuries which Astley's troop could inflict as horses' hooves struck sparks on the minute stages of country playhouses. Henry Thornton's company at Oxford refused to perform unless the actors received an increase of pay to compensate for the inconvenience and danger incurred. They were sacked to a man: that was the price of spectacle.[40]

There is a perversity in human nature which takes a horrified pleasure in watching scenes of catastrophe. In the years in which spectacle was gelling as a composite art on stage, machinists were working on techniques of creating the disintegration of the stage picture. This trait originated in the fires and explosions caused

Pollock's characters from *The Miller and his Men.* (*Author's Collection.*)

by fighters storming 'mediaeval' stage castles. It found its apogee in 1813 in the final moments of Isaac Pocock's melodrama *The Miller and His Men* when Grindoff's mill exploded to provide an 'astonishing and even terrific object'.[41] The play contained those elements of the gothic formula guaranteed to appeal to a mass audience. Banditti lurked in the countryside around Grindoff's mill. The miller was the brigands' chieftain, grinding wheat by day and leading, with amazing stamina, his double life at night. Several stock scenes, the dark forest and the dank cavern, the home of the brigands, met the audiences' expectations but the final scene, although designed on a well-tested pattern, offered a new excitement in the form of a solid, naturalistic windmill, placed in the centre of the stage. John Henderson Grieve and Charles Pugh, the scene-painters, combined with the Covent Garden machinist, Saul, under Farley's direction, to provide the spectacular ending to the play.[42] Toy theatre scenes give an indication of the setting: a bridge led to the mill, which stood slightly elevated on a rock surrounded by water.[43] The layout was reminiscent of a scaled-

A crude but popular print of the 'blow-up' in *The Miller and his Men.* (*Author's Collection.*)

down castle keep protected by its moat and drawbridge. Pocock's stage direction was deceptively simple:

> *Ravina instantly sets fire to the fuze, the flash of which is seen to run down the side of the rock into the gully under the bridge from which she has ascended, and the explosion immediately takes place* (2.5).

The effects of Ravina's action may be seen in a coloured engraving: the upper storey of the mill disintegrated into the borders, a rift appeared in the facade of the building, flames and smoke poured from the truncated structure and, exciting touch, stage-hands catapulted banditti rag-dolls over the top of the ruin. Here was a blow-up to strike terror into hearts previously left unperturbed by lumbering elephants and charging horses. No longer was it sufficient to terminate a play with platitudes couched in rhymed couplets, for in this spectacular explosion could be witnessed the manifestation of the disintegration of evil. Some might find sublimity in the sight.

The elaborate spectacles mentioned in this and earlier chapters point to the need for a sole person to co-ordinate the work of designers, painters, machinists and actors. Unfortunately, for much of the period under survey, no such person came to the fore. As early a gothic play as *Douglas* provided no visual challenges and critics made no comments on the scenery, presumably because it was nondescript. The play's scenic requirements, a castle, a court-yard and a wood, could easily be met from stock. The choice of costumes was left to Spranger Barry and Peg Woffington, the play's two principals. Two foreigners drew the attention of managers to the need for a design co-ordinator; these were Jean Georges Noverre and Philippe Jacques de Loutherbourg. Primarily Nov-verre's province was that of opera and ballet, and he exercised little direct influence on the gothic drama.[44] de Loutherbourg, how-ever, made several proposals to David Garrick at the time of his management of Drury Lane which, in the course of time, influenced spectacular plays such as *Pizarro*, and later, *The Miller and His Men*.[45] He would take charge of 'all which concerns the decorations and machines dependent upon them, the way of lighting them and their manipulation'; he would, too, devise the scenes and prepare them for the painter as well as designing appropriate costumes for dancers and actors. During his time at Drury Lane, from 1773 until 1781, he designed only one of the gothic plays, *Zoraida*, an oriental tale by William Hodgson staged in December 1779.[46] After de Loutherbourg's departure neither Thomas Greenwood at Drury Lane nor John Inigo Richards at Covent Garden enjoyed the same overall responsibility for harmonising the work of the various departments. Indeed, the persons who succeeded in establishing the firmest control over the productions were the acting managers, John Philip Kemble at Drury Lane and Charles Farley at Covent Garden, a heavy responsibility for men who had also to appear on stage.

de Loutherbourg's interest lay in depicting the wildness of nature, which he did in studio paintings and on the stage. As the former included such subjects as smugglers caught in coastal storms or the lonely encampments of a group of banditti, material derived from Salvator Rosa, it is surprising that de Loutherbourg contri-buted so little to gothic stage presentations.[47] His experiments in

Philippe Jacques de Loutherbourg by Thomas Gainsborough. (*By permission of the Governors of Dulwich Picture Gallery.*)

87

the Eidophusikon with contrasting effects of light and darkness would seem to have made him an ideal designer for this genre and gothic staging was the poorer without his vibrant, imaginative output and technical expertise.

As the gothic dramas developed, so the conditions in which the plays were performed altered. Richard Cumberland observed that both the patent houses became 'theatres for spectators rather than playhouses for hearers' from the 1790s.[48] Before the change to larger stages and auditoria spectacles had become an important part of presentation: the trend is exemplified in *Richard, Coeur de Lion, The Battle of Hexham* and *The Crusade.* By 1794 the machinist had become so invaluable in the preparation of spectacle that, in rebuilding Drury Lane, Henry Holland invited Rudolph Cabanel of Lambeth to prepare plans for the machines, basing them on the necessities of the opening production of *Macbeth* on the supposition that this production would serve as a model for the requirements of others.[49] In order to speed the scene changes, arrangements were made for wings and shutters to be flown upwards or lowered through sloats in the stage floor, in addition to their conventional horizontal movement. Posts erected in the wings for side lighting were an important feature of the new house. At the same time Thomas Harris of Covent Garden, not to be outdone by Sheridan at the Lane, engaged Holland to effect a restructuring of his theatre; however, as the work was completed at a fraction of the expenditure of its rival, few mechanical innovations were added to the stage area.[50] The size of the auditorium of Drury Lane greatly increased and was to do so again at both theatres in 1809 (Covent Garden) and 1812 (Drury Lane). No longer could the 'moving brow and penetrating eye' of the performer be seen throughout the house.[51] Acting became externalised and highly flamboyant performances were needed in order to project characters to the distant audience. Spectacle at this point came into its own with the two great gothic presentations of the decade, *The Miller and His Men* at Covent Garden and *The Falls of Clyde* at Drury Lane. It must, however, be remembered that there were frequent revivals of earlier plays and these were occasionally reworked into spectacles to cater for current taste. The arrival of Edmund Kean ensured that revivals of specific roles, such as De Monfort and Sir Edward Mortimer, were similarly reworked: he moved away from the statuesque performances of members of the Kemble school and, although lacking in inches, he filled the stage with the dynamics of his personality.

Little is known of the details of lighting individual plays. Prompt books tended to give merely the signal 'Lamps Down', indicating a lowering of the oil lamps below the proscenium level which caused the front stage to darken. The use of shadow as well as light has been noted in several instances. The mysterious quality of light and shade was temporarily lost at Drury Lane in 1816 when gas lighting was installed, and Lord Byron's cynical assertion that it would 'poison half the audience and all the *dramatis personae*' was found to be incorrect.[52] A row of eighty lamps fronted the proscenium and twelve lines of lamps were fitted in the wings. Joanna Baillie commented that gas gave a 'full, staring, uniform light', ruining the atmosphere of tragedy.[53] Although the alternations of light and shade which the theatre had previously enjoyed were lost for a while, it became possible to regulate the overall intensity of the light with much greater precision. Moreover, the gas could be used to express changes of emotion. *The Tale of Mystery* was revived immediately after the gas was introduced. At the beginning of the storm scene the lights were dimmed but on Romaldi's joyful sighting of Michelli, in spite of the continuing tempest, they were raised to signify the uplifting of Romaldi's spirits.[54] It was a small touch but prior to 1816 the only auxiliary indication of such a change of atmosphere was the music. It was a wonder that, in a genre so suffused with emotion, the use of music throughout the play as a commentary on feeling was not seriously considered until the beginning of the nineteenth century and that those in charge of the *mise-en-scène* were deprived of flexibility in the lighting equipment until the second decade of the century. Both were, and still are, a gift in the hands of a director wishing to make an overt statement about the inner lives of the characters he is presenting.

Chapter Five: Attitude and Speech

Gothic drama did not demand from the actor a special style of performance. Indeed, as we have seen, there was no such clearly demarcated category of play. The ordinary acting conventions of the eighteenth-century stage pertained. Two gothic roles which enjoyed a number of revivals are used as case studies in this chapter but before addressing ourselves to them some consideration of performance on the Georgian stage, whatever the genre of the play, must be made.

In a letter to James Boaden, Benjamin Haydon remarked of Sarah Siddons's acting style that she 'seemed always to throw herself on Nature as a guide, and follow instantaneously what she suggested'.[1] To follow nature, however, was not to replicate slavishly the behaviour of the every-day world. It was a matter of selection and refinement. Joshua Reynolds in his discourses to the Royal Academy referred on several occasions to the actor and revealed an understanding of his art. The following sentences of Reynolds add to our understanding of the concept of Nature mentioned by Haydon:

> Nature, then, in the sense in which it is imitated, must signify not the conclusive, mean appearance of natural phenomena, but rather what we might wish there to be, or – identifying human desire with the will of the Creator – the otherwise unfulfilled intentions of God. This means that art must imitate the *ideal* world and not the *real*.[2]

If the portrayal on stage of emotion or passion was to be an idealisation, how was this to be achieved? In his portraits – whether of opera singers or admirals – Reynolds regarded the pose adopted by figures in high renaissance painting as both an idealisation of nature and also as indicative of a conventionalisation of the portrayal of an emotion. In Reynolds's painting of Sarah Siddons as 'The Tragic Muse', for example, Siddons's pose representing melancholy has its origin in Michaelangelo's figure of Isaiah in the Sistine Chapel, and Reynolds thereby uses the Isaiah pose as a physical codification of melancholy.[3] These codified poses were to be found in actors' manuals: that written by Mrs Siddons's son, Henry, adapted from J. J. Engel, serves as an example.[4] In *Practical Illustrations of Rhetorical Gesture and Action* a number of stances signifying such emotions as suspicion, terror, expectation and sublime adoration were illustrated. Incidentally these illustrations reflect the attitudes adopted by members of the Kemble family. Lest the poses should become mechanical, Henry Siddons gave the basic advice that the actor should 'seize all occasions of observing nature' but with the proviso that in performance he should avoid giving his audience 'too coarse or too servile an imitation of the source'.[5] It appears that the actor held each attitude for a length of time as he delivered his lines, changing the pose as he became gripped by a new emotion. This is consistent with the attitudes shown in manuals and in engravings: the weight was placed on one leg; a wide stance using as much personal space as was workable was adopted; one hand articulated at some point of the body, whilst the free hand and arm broadly described the space around the actor.[6] Thus the attitude may root the actor temporarily to the deck of the stage but his adopted stance allowed for grand gesture, which led to Mrs Crawford's waspish comment that the performances of the Kemble school, in contrast to David Garrick's more restrained and instinctive acting, were 'all paw and pause'.[7] Here was the 'grace of attitude' of which William Stone spoke approvingly in his treatise on acting.[8]

Mrs Crawford's criticism could be mitigated by the actor's habit of infusing certain highlights in the play with an amazing dynamism, thus creating an alternation of a series of static tableaux with an interlude of intense activity. Audiences awaited these moments in the play with expectation and responded to the performer's virtuosity with sobbing, applause or shrieks. These

(*left*) Sarah Siddons rehearsing in the green-room with her father, Roger Kemble, and, in the background, John Henderson; a drawing by Thomas Rowlandson. (*Theatre Collection, University of Bristol.*)

(*right*) Charles Farley as Francisco the deaf mute in *A Tale of Mystery*; Farley's stance illustrates the spacious boldness of the Georgian stage attitude. (*Maugham Collection, Royal National Theatre.*)

galvanisations are set within descriptions of performances of *Douglas*, *The Castle Spectre* and *Pizarro* in the case studies of the following chapter. Lest the impression is given that a galvanisation was merely an athletic interlude, it must be stressed that it was an intensification to an emotional breaking point of one's perform-ance; it might be as simple in its expression as the long-held gaze which the heroine of *Percy* (Hannah More, 1777) maintained:

> The dumb despair of Miss Young was, in the expression of countenance, superior to all the power of eloquence; and produced such an effect on the audience, as I do not remember ever to have seen. Her look to Guildford her father, when she pronounced these simple words, 'Methinks your daughter should not have been refused', throbbed every heart and drew tears from every eye.[9]

The heroine presented a spectacle of pathos, to which the audience responded with pity, overtly expressing its emotion in unashamed tears.

In addition to the 'grace of attitude', Stone wrote of the 'art of speech'. The rapidity of speaking which characterised the Garrick school gave way to measured speech which was judged to be the proper delivery for the language of tragedy and an actor was condemned if he were 'a casual repeater of blank verse', as Thomas Morris found John Henderson to be.[10] 'Henderson cared little about the measure of a line,' wrote Boaden, 'he would not consider the fame of the versifier while the heart was to be struck.'[11] Poor Henderson was in much the same situation as Robert Mahon performing in *The Countess of Salisbury* in Cork. The local newspaper castigated his vocal lightness with the condemnation that he was 'totally incapable of [speaking] blank verse'.[12]

A German visitor, Georg Foster, noted that the speech of the Georgian stage was 'very precise, very pure and distinct'; it tended to be declaimed, but, he added, it stopped short of becoming a song.[13] Kemble and his followers battened their stage speech on to metrical and rhythmical stresses; by this means they idealised tragic diction.[14] Of course, one could hammer the stresses and so produce the monotonous performance Boaden described:

> ... if the ACTOR forces [the blank verse] into a song, and either *moans* it out in a uniform chant, or *parades* his words like military steps, in slow, quick, or double-quick time, as they tend to excite attention, or vehement applause to himself, he will interpret truly neither NATURE nor his AUTHOR, but stamp his own character as a *mannerist* ...[15]

Sometimes playwrights expected the metre to be stressed. Sheridan, as performers rehearsed his tragedy *Pizarro*, '[counted] poetically the measure upon his fingers, and [sounded] with his voice like a music master'. Boaden discovered the reason:

> Sheridan's ear was made up to this artificial cadence in the drama. His own declamation was of the old school; and when you read either his *School for Scandal* or his *Critic*, you discover the *tune* to which, like a composer, he had set every line in them.[16]

Whereas the stage speech of Siddons and Kemble delighted Sheri-

(*left*) Richard III played by Edmund Kean, a physically slight actor whose dynamism filled the stage and helped to displace the powerful influence of the Kemble family. (*George Speaight.*)

(*right*) Sarah Siddons as Euphrasia in *The Grecian Daughter* drawn by Mary Hamilton during the actress's Dublin visist in 1802; the simplicity of her costume in this drawing may be compared with the heavily elaborate one depicted on page 74. (*Reproduced by courtesy of the Trustees of the British Museum.*)

dan, the informal, ebullient speech of Mrs Jordan exasperated the playwright.[17]

It was left to Kean to destroy the self-conscious mannerisms of the 'Kemble religion'.[18] Within the athleticism of his performance, unattainable by Kemble because of his respiratory handicaps, there was no room for self-conscious attitudes or mannered speaking. Contrasting the styles of the two men in the role of Sir Edward Mortimer (*The Iron Chest*), Hazlitt wrote:

> [Kemble] is the statue on the pedestal, that cannot come down without shaming its worshippers; a figure that tells well with appropriate scenery and dresses; but not otherwise ... He minds only the conduct of his own person, and leaves the piece to shift for itself. Not so Mr Kean. 'Truly he hath a devil;' and if the fit comes over him too often, yet, as tragedy is not the representation of *still-life*, we think this much better than never being roused at all.[19]

94

But even Kean could wryly admit that on occasions his Satanic explosions could reduce speech to an indistinct 'bow-wow-wow'.[20]

In order to root these observations within the gothic drama, two roles have been selected as case studies in which the approach of performers may be observed. The roles are those of Euphrasia in *The Grecian Daughter* and De Monfort in the play of the same name.

The Grecian Daughter is a monodrama and its central role offered great scope to the actress, indeed David Garrick referred to the part of Euphrasia as 'one of the finest ... in all the dramatic circle'.[21] Writing more than half a century later than Garrick, John Galt described the part as one of those 'which young actresses think necessary to go through before they consider their reputation established'.[22] In 1782 Sarah Siddons, then twenty-seven years old, took the part from Mrs Yates and continued to play it throughout her long career. In her early portrayals Siddons stressed the dignified repose of the character. Almost thirty years later Louis Simond, an occasional visitor from America, saw her and declared that with 'fewer natural advantages her talents remain the same, and she is certainly a very great actress', a remark which suggested that her performance, in its objectivity, had transcended age, as Barry's had in portraying the young Norval.[23] Siddons's physical presence had developed with the added years, making her a tall and commanding figure, although, wrote Boaden, she remained 'always feminine'.[24] Another attribute was the marked structure of her face which ensured that her expression was evident to many people in the enlarging patent houses. Actresses such as Mrs Robinson had failed in the role claimed Tate Wilkinson for, although their speaking of the verse might be pleasing, they lacked the strong definition of feature to be a successful tragic actress.[25]

Several incidents in Siddons's performance of Euphrasia were singled out for comment by her audiences: there was the climax of the play in which the heroine stabbed Dionysius, the usurper-tyrant; there was also Euphrasia's defence of the reputation of her son, Phocion, and her grief when she learnt of the supposed death of her father, Evander. In contrast to her general stillness, at such points her playing became galvanised. In the last-mentioned of these highlights the setting was a wild romantic landscape of rocks and caverns. So great was Euphrasia's sorrow that she over-projected the lines, causing the spectators to envisage her 'standing on the cliff in madness and despair':

> This is my last abode – these caves, these rocks,
> Shall ring for ever with Euphrasia's wrongs: . . .
> Here will I dwell and rave, and shriek, and give
> These scattered locks to all the passing winds.[26]

This, Campbell wrote in his biography of the actress, was to portray filial sorrow 'with a terrible fidelity'.[27] By the fourth act of the play Euphrasia's son, Phocion, had surrounded the walls of Syracuse; Dionysius demanded that Euphrasia should use her influence with her son to break the siege. Euphrasia's reply was instant:

> Think'st thou then
> So meanly of my Phocion? Dost thou deem him
> Poorly wound up to a mere fit of valour
> To melt away in a weak woman's tear?
> O thou dost little know him (4.1).

Her second question was asked so passionately that, reported a spectator, 'everyone who hears her is persuaded that she is perfectly capable in real life of acting the part she here only personates and they admire the woman even more than the actress'.[28] Boaden recorded that she went on to speak of the purpose and virtue of her son with a triumph and enjoyment which was 'electrical', causing the audience to break into a full minute's applause.[29] Much of the time Siddons may have been static but there were episodes when she blazed with vitality to which the audience responded joyously.

Siddons confessed to Mrs Piozzi that the role of Euphrasia demanded 'violent exertion' of her, to the point that she injured her side after stabbing the tyrant in order to save her father who was about to be executed.[30] The killing was a strange action, certainly out of key with the heroine's characteristics, and this appeared to be reflected in Siddons's performance. Captain Friedrich von Hassell described it as 'an anxious thrust of the dagger . . . and the unfamiliar weapon glides at the very same moment from her trembling fingers'.[31] When she saw her father safe and the enemy dead 'what emotions followed one another

MRS SIDDONS

In defending her father Euphrasia was in danger of abdicating from her role of the heroine: Matthew Gregory Lewis had to append a footnote to the text of *Adelgitha* explaining that the principal female character, who also slew a tyrant, was not in fact the heroine of his piece. (*Author's Collection.*)

in her features'. She sank to her knees, stretching upward the arm which had thrust the knife and maintained this attitude for five minutes. All possible pathos was wrung from the scene to the extent that 'on all sides nothing was to be heard save sobbing and soft applause'. This was an attitude which passed into theatrical lore and, wishing to describe the appearance of Mrs Rivers making an apology, Tate Wilkinson referred to her gesture as 'with arm uplifted like the Grecian Daughter in the last act'.[32]

The interpretation of Siddons may be compared with that of Ann Barry who played the part in the first production. A spectator gave his impression:

> Euphrasia was . . . sustained throughout with great ability; all that firmness and constancy in the hour of danger – all that sweet solicitude for her father's safety and existence, were portrayed with such a true and feminine expression as all acknowledged and all repaid with their tears.[33]

Barry showed none of Siddons's reticence in slaying the tyrant. Each night there was a whole-hearted physical involvement in the action, so much so that when on one occasion the spring of the blade jammed John Palmer, playing Dionysius, was confined to bed for five months.[34] This involvement of Barry's was spasmodic. On a further occasion as she was about to wield the dagger, she heard one of the temple attendants giggling and delayed the attack until she had admonished her. A strange impropriety on the part of both women.[35]

Siddons was highly acclaimed in the role by her audiences and yet, said Thomas Dutton, he preferred Mrs Powell's Euphrasia because her acting was emotive and impulsive, a contrast to the 'studied and monotonous manner of Mrs Siddons', which he found the same in every character and situation.[36] The two actresses represented contrasts in style. Siddons was the idealist; Mrs Powell, belonging to a new generation, marked the change to instinctive performance.[37]

The second case study is based on the role of De Monfort. It has already been mentioned that Joanna Baillie wrote *De Monfort* as part of a scheme to show the effects of a mastering passion on a key character.[38] Hate was the defect of De Monfort – he hated Rezenfelt, his acquaintance from childhood. In this play, Baillie unfortunately created difficulties for her hero: the drama tended to be an interior one, allowing for little stage action.[39] Several writers, Anna Seward of Lichfield and the playwright, Elizabeth Inchbald, among them, felt that Rezenfelt was a gentle and amiable person, impossible to hate, with the result that De Monfort appeared as a 'pitiable maniac'.[40] Baillie's anonymous editor pointed to the principal defect in the thrust of the play in his statement that the author 'proposed to render her plots subservient to her main end, the development of one dominant and overreaching passion'.[41]

Under pressure from his sister, who was interested in the role of Lady Jane De Monfort, Kemble agreed to take the lead. Baillie was delighted: in her delineation of the character she had envisaged Kemble playing the part and had incorporated into it those set pieces – the statuesque and, in contrast, the sudden burst of energy and passion – which were the hallmark of performances by the Kembles.[42] The self-divided character bore some resemblance to Macbeth which Kemble had already played with acclaim. He mastered intellectually the compexity of De Monfort's disintegration, giving it, said Hazlitt, 'a sense of purpose and a precision of outline'.[43] Unfortunately he had to work against the Rezenfelt of a light-weight actor, Montagu Talbot, which detracted from his fire.[44]

Baillie's stage directions guided the actor in his portrayal. The externalisation of his villainous character was commonplace:

Enter De Monfort with his Arms crossed, with a thoughtful frowning Aspect, and passes slowly across the stage . . . (3.3).

This was an entry which three years earlier the Earl Osmond (*The Castle Spectre*) had made. At the mention or appearance of Rezenfelt his volatile nature was observable in his actions:

De Monfort walks up and down impatiently and irresolute; at last he pulls the Bell violently (1.2).

Passion and remorse were to be expressed strongly. After Rezenfelt's murder De Monfort stood *fix'd and motionless with horror* until the corpse was uncovered when *a sudden shivering seem[ed] to pass over him* (4.3). Appalled by the enormity of his crime, he furiously rammed his head against one of the walls of the convent wishing for death. Reflecting on the role and envisaging his uncle's interpretation, Henry Siddons described the demeanour of the character:

> ...his gait is as vague and as uncertain as his countenance. He is perpetually varying his attitudes, and he keeps continually rubbing his forehead, as if he wished to efface from his memory the last trace of the thought which thus afflicts him.[45]

Unlike her contemporaries, Baillie gave no directions about the facial reactions necessary for portraying De Monfort. Her expectation that Kemble would take the role would make these superfluous. However, she did realise the necessity for the actor's face to be clearly visible to the audience, a point which few gothic playwrights, setting many scenes in melancholy gloom, seemed to consider. Baillie had admired the contrast in oil paintings, especially those of Rosa, in which the light from a camp fire had picked out the faces of gypsies and banditti, leaving the background in total darkness.[46] But in the theatre the actor's face suffered in the glow of the footlights for 'every feature immediately [became] shortened and snub and less capable of any expression'.[47] She tried to obviate this disadvantage. De Monfort was dragged to the front of a darkened stage by monks who had found him near the corpse of Rezenfelt. Each monk carried a lantern by means of which, at a strategic moment, De Monfort's face was lit:

> *As they lead forward De Monfort, Light is turned away, so that he is seen obscurely but when they come to the Front of the Stage, they turn the Light Side of their Lanterns on him at once, and his Face is seen in all the Strengthened Horror and Despair, with his Hands and Clothes bloody* (4.3).

Other than in their use of flaming brands, few playwrights had attempted to exploit the use of localised lighting in their creation of a dark scene of horror.

In his soliloquies De Monfort laid bare the turmoil of his mind. Possibly Baillie thought of Kemble's solemn delivery when she expressed her fear that the soliloquies would be given by an actor 'as if he were addressing some person whom it behoved him to

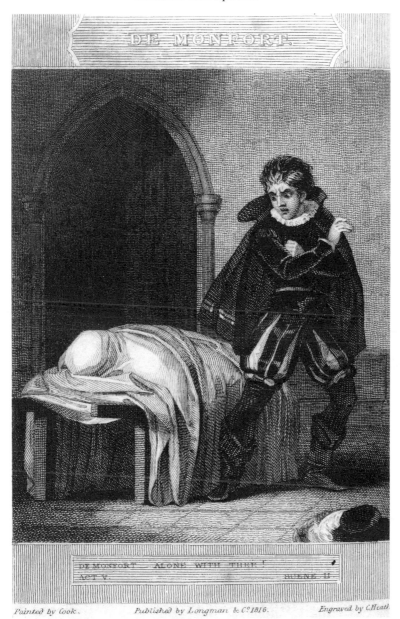

De Monfort (initially played by John Philip Kemble) alone with the body of Rezenvenvelt whom he has jealously slain. (*Bodleian Library, Oxford (M adds III f 151).*)

treat with great ceremony ... in an audible, uniform voice'.[48] Baillie suggested that a soliloquy was the heavily suppressed 'musing of a perturbed mind' and to become alive in the theatre the speaking of it needed 'that rapid burst of sounds which often succeeds the slow, languid tones of distress; those sudden, untuned exclamations, which, as if frightened at their own discord, are struck again into silence as sudden and abrupt'.[49] In consequence, the playwright gave detailed instructions on the performance of the soliloquies. A look at one in the third act will make clear her intentions. De Monfort had been informed that Rezenfelt planned to marry his sister, Lady Jane, and as she and Rezenfelt strolled in the garden De Monfort watched them through the doorway. Before the start of the soliloquy Baillie noted that the actor was to *come forward to the Front of the Stage, and make a long Pause, expressive of some great Agony of Mind* (3.3). As he pondered on the relationship between the couple his distress was to increase visibly. To demonstrate this he would throw himself into a chair and, covering his face with his hands, burst into tears. Suddenly he would start up from his seat furiously, a change of attitude prompted by a new line of thought, for he spoke no longer of his distress at the projected marriage, but of his revenge on Rezenfelt. Suiting action to words he took his dagger and, imagining that he saw Rezenfelt's form in the room, he hurled the weapon at it. Moments later Rezenfelt in reality entered the room, by which time pent up emotion burst into activity:

> *De Monfort turns round, and on seeing him starts but then, drawing his sword, rushed furiously upon him.*

This soliloquy was a progression of thought, clearly defined and divided into four sections, each punctuated by a decisive action and increasing in frenzy.

The role of De Monfort suited Kemble. Hazlitt described him as 'the very still-life and statuary of the stage; a perfect figure of a man; a petrification of a sentiment ...', and, as such, an eminently suitable actor to deal with the slow reflective verse of the first three acts.[50] He possessed positive qualities: Sir Walter Scott remarked that he was a 'lordly vessel, goodly and magnificent when going large before the wind'.[51] He could, too, comprehend and translate into a clear and unified performance emotions which lay beneath the surface. John Taylor expressed this:

> Hence oft we see him with success explore,
> And clear the dross from rich poetic ore;
> Trace through the maze of diction passions's clew,
> And open latent character to view.[52]

Furthermore, he was adept in charging his performance with dynamism, although only for limited periods, to the terror and delight of the audience. It was in his speaking of the role that Kemble was at his weakest. Although his diction was clear, he was hindered by asthma and a habitual cough. These indispositions were responsible for the painful 'Kemble pause' ('He speaks so slow,' complained Sheridan to Lord Duncannon, 'He ought to make the orchestra play between each word . . .') and for the 'eternal groan' spliced into his speeches.[53] Vocal production could not keep pace with the force of passion he attempted to express, with the result that modulation became inflexible.[54] It was doubly unfortunate that Sarah Siddons, without the excuse of respiratory difficulties, fell into similar vocal mannerisms. Acting together in *De Monfort* the two performers would, in Anthony Pasquin's phrase, produce the 'same ahs, same ohs, the same starts, the same groans . . .'[55]

Twenty years later Lord Byron, anxious to raise the standard of drama at Drury Lane, invited Edmund Kean to stage a revival of Baillie's play. Kean lacked the dignified stature of Kemble but, in compensation, he was gifted with limitless energy. In performance those episodes in which De Monfort brooded on his sister's love for Rezenfelt were 'really terrific' and the preparations for Rezenfelt's murder 'surpassed in speechless delineation anything of this kind ever seen on the stage'.[56] Under Kean's guidance Baillie restructured the final act of the play which, she felt, made it 'better fitted for exhibition'.[57] The principal change involved leaving De Monfort alone with the corpse at the end of the play so that, having made his final speech, Kean threw himself to the ground as the curtain fell.[58] Sitting in the dress circle of Drury Lane at the revival, the playwright enthusiastically expressed her satisfaction with Kean's interpretation.[59]

Too often gothic dramas have been dismissed by critics who have lacked the knowledge of Georgian acting skills to recognise that the texts were blue prints for performance, requiring a specifically technical realisation. When the texts are re-examined in the light of their performers' response, it is evident that many a playwright had current styles of performance firmly in mind and utilised these in telling his story. We have already looked at the rapidly changing scenes which were a feature of most gothic plays and gave them flexibility; against that flux performers produced alternations of stationary attitude and galvanic activity, revealing the highlights and climaxes dormant in the text. The audience responded enthusiastically to interpretation, awaiting those points of the play which merited an overt expression of terror, grief, laughter or compassion. Such conventions as the direct address and the aside made actors and audience sensitively aware of each other. The audience was an integral part of the performance of the play. This unison and appreciation of acting style may help to explain the audience's acceptance of a performance as an objective statement of a role and its easy reception of such apparent infelicities as the disparity which often existed between the age of the actor and the character he played. Without the Kemble school's emphasis on the technical mastery of one's art, the credibility of many a characterisation would have crumbled. Acceptability was aided, too, by the stock nature of many of the roles. However, unless the role was infused by the performer with genuine inner life, it remained merely a cipher in the plot and not a living entity. Technical mastery, although highly important, was not enough; it was necessary that the actor breathed life into his role.

It is worth remembering that the art of acting is always in a state of transition, but the speed of its change varies. Although a gap of thirty years separated *The Grecian Daughter* from *De Monfort*, descriptions of incidents in each of the plays suggest that a common acting style was employed. The performances of the Kembles were, in part, a reaction against the naturalism which David Garrick initiated at Drury Lane; in turn Edmund Kean reacted against the studied artifice of the Kemble school which had preceded his own era and plays other than *De Monfort* were also subjected to a degree of rewriting in order to accommodate stylistic changes. Thus, both ideally and practically, writing, performance and reception were interdependent in a successful stage realisation as we shall consider in the case studies of the next chapter.

Chapter Six: Three Case Studies

Nowadays it is impossible to apprehend fully the reasons for the popularity of the gothic drama if we think of the constituents of text, design and acting as separate elements. Ideally these should be fused together into a performance so that the qualities of excitement and escapism which the plays offered their audiences could be appreciated. The best that can be done is to describe the staging of several gothic plays in the hope that something of the magic of the total performance may be glimpsed. Georgian critics frequently pointed out that during a successful gothic drama the audience was carried along by enthusiasm for the piece; disbelief, indeed the critical evaluative process, were laid aside for the evening as music, colour and flamboyant histrionics held the attention. It is in this enthusiastic spirit that the following case studies of *Douglas*, *The Castle Spectre* and *Pizarro* are offered to the reader.

The latter two plays the author has directed and he can vouch for the theatrical viability of their power still to hold an audience. *Douglas* is an example of an early gothic drama. It offered little by way of stage spectacle: scenery was minimal, opportunities for massed groupings of costumed actors did not arise. Nevertheless, excitement could be found in performance. The span of time the play was kept in the repertoire, a hundred years, enabled theatregoers to compare the highlights of one actor's portrayal with another and to respond overtly with approbation or, occasionally, displeasure. These comparisons made for an air of anticipation in the auditorium and helped to link spectators and actors in a bond based on their common appreciation of performance style.

Some fifty years separated *Douglas* from the other two plays, which were in turn performed within three years of each other. *The Castle Spectre* is an example of a gothic melodrama, a Georgian morality play. Written by Matthew Lewis, it was a highly conservative example of playwriting at the time with its stress on the supernatural and on the ultimate triumph of virtue over lust. *Pizarro*, too, was about virtue; it was also about the morals of politics as understood by Richard Sheridan, himself a Whig Member of Parliament. In Sheridan's day the play worked on a political level, which can only be appreciated today in the light of programme notes. What does remain is the opportunity for spectacle in both settings and the massed effect of the supernumaries; also for the flamboyant portrayal of Sheridan's larger-than-life characters with their vigour and ability to deal dynamically with the situations in which they found themselves. Here was spectacle on an extensive scale undreamt of by John Home when he wrote *Douglas*. Public taste, changing styles of acting and, above all, the development of theatrical design, were responsible for the evolution. The constant factor offered by the three plays lay not on the stage but in the auditorium, – the enthusiasm of the audience's response. The disapproval expressed when an audience found a play or a performer wanting could be conveyed equally strongly. However, the plays in these three case-studies were highly successful on the London stage.

John Home's play, *Douglas*, received its first London performance at Covent Garden on 14 March 1757. Many in the audience were aware that the play had already been given professional performances, received with acclaim, in Edinburgh during the previous year.[1] The publication of the text, on the other hand, had gained a mixed reception.[2] Most periodicals approved but the *Critical Review* complained that the dialogue, which Home had attempted to make 'a pattern of true simplicity', was undistinguished and at times banal.[3] Other writers welcomed the 'pastoral simplicity' of Home's style, finding that it contained 'an easy strength'.[4] Audiences may have known that prior to the Scottish production David Garrick had turned down the opportunity to stage the play at Drury Lane, complaining of its lack of action (the plot was

narrated in lengthy set speeches) and fearing that his company
would be faced with the impossibility of 'raising the Passions or
comanding [*sic*] attention'.[5]

In spite of these reservations two stars of the London stage
appeared in the Covent Garden production: Peg Woffington made
one of the last appearances of her career as Lady Randolph and
Spranger Barry, whose voice was reputed to be the most mellifluous
on the stage, at the age of thirty-eight played the teen-age Norval.
The Prologue warned the audience that it was to witness a 'she-
tragedy':

> This night a Douglas your protection claims;
> A wife! a mother! Pity's softest names:
> The story of her woes indulgent hear,
> And grant your suppliant all she begs, a tear.

Beyond the rising curtain the courtyard of a castle surrounded
by woodland came into view. Lady Randolph entered through the
proscenium doors and from the start of her performance broke
'into a beautiful Pathos, at once poetical and simple' noted Arthur
Murphy.[6]

She presented to the audience a gothic theme, that of the lost
relative supposed dead: sixteen years earlier her husband had been
killed in battle and her infant son lost when his nurse had attempted
to take him through a winter storm to the safety of her sister's
house. As Woffington performed the manager of the Canongate
Theatre in Edinburgh, who had travelled to London to see the
performance, was entranced by this actress who 'looked and moved
the character she represented most divinely'.[7] Her only disadvantage was a harshness of tone in her voice. This was a far cry from
Tate Wilkinson's satiric description of Mrs Robinson's opening
scene:

> ...she appeared to an universal greeting and a remarkably genteel
> audience in the character of Lady Randolph, and after the awful
> descent, and usual ceremony of a loud applause and a courtesy – again
> repeated – a sigh and another applause – according to the fashion
> after a few tears, the use of the white handkerchief, a tremble, a totter,
> a short retirement to cruel grief, all such ceremonies being adjusted,
> Lady Randolph gazed, and after pronouncing faintly and tremulously:
> Ye woods and wilds, whose melancholy sounds

Pollock's characters in *Douglas*; Siddons's choice of coronet and veil is picked up in this representation of Lady Randolph. (*Author's Collection.*)

> Accord with my soul's sadness,
> the vibration and articulation strengthened by degrees, and all went
> on smooth and quiet, with three good attendants, silence, attention
> and applause.[8]

Lady Randolph received news that Glenalvon, the villain Home had cast in the mould of Iago and the instigator of the heroine's miseries, was approaching. The physical appearance of Glenalvon presented the actor with a problem, for a highland costume seemed inappropriate for the villain. At Barry's former theatre in Crow Street, Dublin, one, Barrett, had played the role dressed, according to John Bernard, in an entire suit of black, with a black wig (the mark of a villain) and a black velvet hat adorned with plumes of black feathers.[9] Avoiding this traditional garb of the villain, Francis Aickin, who played the role in 1783, appeared as if he were 'designed for the soft service of Venus'.[10] Glenalvon had previously made a protestation of love to Lady Randolph and she had threatened to acquaint her second husband of his passion. In the soliloquy which ended the act there was a fearsome simplicity in Glenalvon's statement: 'Randolph has liv'd too long'.

Glenalvon's soliloquies punctuated the first three acts of the play as if they were choric odes in a classical tragedy. Possibly some of the audience realised that each act resembled an *episodion* in which a new character appeared on whom the subsequent dialogue hinged. In the second act this was the figure of Norval, a teenage lad, who confronted with open honesty Lord and Lady Randolph. 'I was most forcibly struck with Mr Barry in the Young Hero,' whote John Jackson. 'I must indeed have been devoid of every spark of sensation if I had sat an unaffected spectator.'[11] Tate Wilkinson, however, whilst admitting that Barry's performance was an enjoyable one, found that his figure, well-made and over six feet in height, was unsuitable for representing the stripling and 'he looked the worse for having decorated the simple shepherd in a rich, puckered white satin shape'.[12] The young lad's opening words became a standard excerpt for would-be actors to recite at provincial spouting-clubs:

> My Name is Norval: on the Grampian hills
> My father feeds his flocks; a frugal swain,
> Whose constant cares were to increase his store,
> And keep his only son, myself, at home.

The part of Norval was played with acclaim by the juvenile phenomenon Willian Henry West Betty during the 1804–05 season at Covent Garden.[13] He was then fourteen and Douglas was a role more suited to his slight physique and pretty demeanour than those of Hamlet and Richard III which he also performed. Dorothy Wordsworth wrote on this subject to Lady Beaumont: 'I do not think that there is anything in the character of Douglas ... which a boy of great talents might not be able to comprehend and conceive'.[14] William Hazlitt watched the encounter between son and mother:

> ... he seemed almost like 'some gay creature of the element' moving about gracefully, with all the flexibility of youth, and murmuring Aeolian sounds with plaintive tenderness. I shall never forget the way in which he repeated the line in which Young Norval says, speaking of the fate of the two brothers:

Mrs SIDDONS.
AS LADY RANDOLPH IN DOUGLAS

(*left*) Isaac Cruikshank's drawing of Sarah Siddons as Lady Randolph in *Douglas*, an example of both the mature heroine in mourning and of an attitude made impressive by the stature of the actress and her choice of costume. (*Theatre Museum; by courtesy of the Board of Trustees of the Victoria and Albert Museum*).

(*right*) John Opie's painting of William Henry West Betty as Young Norval in *Douglas* seen against a bleak but non-gothic landscape. (*National Portrait Gallery.*)

And in my mind happy was he that died![15]

It was a portrayal which gained the approval of the aged John Home who watched the play from the wings and, in spite of having seen Barry in the role, commended the authenticity of the playing as in accord with his own conception of the part.[16]

With that prescience which is given to tragic heroines, Lady Randolph recognised a kinship between herself and the young man: 'Thou shalt be My Knight,' she said, appointing him to serve Lord Randolph. In the course of time the scene developed into one of the highlights of the play. Mrs Jackson took over the role in 1779. As she gazed at Norval she

> showed in her countenance the inward feelings she afterwards declared to Anna. Her manner of thanking the youth, with her reflection on

                    – The wonder-working hand of Heav'n,
seemed to flow from a pious frame of mind, which adores Providence
in every event; and her chusing him for *her Knight* expressed both
gratitude to him, and a friendly care for Lord Randolph's safety.[17]

Later, in 1811, Sarah Siddons's portrayal of Lady Randolph was
graphically recorded by William Macready who played opposite
her. He described this scene with her lost son:

> ...the mournful admiration of her look, as she fixed her gaze upon
> him, plainly told that the tear which Randolph observed to start in
> her eye was nature's parental instinct in the presence of her son.[18]

The third act introduced Old Norval to the audience, who appeared
as a prisoner and gave an account of his past life. His narration
gained greatly in interest when he told of his discovery of a baby
floating in a basket in the river running past his hovel. Lady Randolph asked an anguished question, brief, but in the stage-history
of *Douglas* one that came to be regarded as a challenge to the
actress: 'Was he alive?'. At the moment of the question Mrs Crawford, who took over the role after Woffington's death, let out a
shriek which, said Bannister, 'made rows of spectators start from
their seats'; it was an effect which, a newspaper writer claimed,
made an appeal to the heart of the spectator.[19] Mrs Jackson was
similarly unrestrained in her enquiry. Her panegyrist recorded:

> During the story of Old Norval, her eye, the different muscles of her
> face, nay her whole frame, seemed to be moved by a variety of conflict-
> ing passions. Curiosity sat on her brow, in company with Doubt and
> Fear. But when he mentioned a child being brought to the river side,
> her maternal curiosity burst out, unrestrained, with the exclamation,
>   – Was he alive?
> This she uttered with the utmost exertion of her voice, her eye wild
> with terror, and her breast heaving with a doubt, that seem'd to fear,
> whilst it eagerly pressed to be resolved.[20]

In the 1780s, when she assumed the part, Sarah Siddons became
wildly agitated during the Stranger's story, accompanying her inter-
jections with 'impassioned gestures' which did away with any
impression of worry, suggesting rather a mental enfeeblement.[21]
She was still making a restless response in 1811 when, according
to Macready, the

violence of her agitation while listening to Old Norval's narration of the perils of her infant seemed beyond her power longer to endure, and the words, faintly articulated, as if the last effort of a mortal agony, 'Was he alive?' sent an electric thrill through the audience.[22]

This quiet intensity of Siddons prompted Thomas Gray to pronounce the scene 'so masterly that it strikes me blind to all its defects.'[23]

The *anagnorisis* – the moment in which the protagonist recognised truth – was achieved in the penultimate act, reinforcing the classical structure of the play: Lady Randolph declared to her son her relationship to him.

A change of location for the final act took the audience to a 'sweet and solemn' wood at midnight. Physical action, in abeyance until this moment, suddenly erupted in the duel of Norval with Glenalvon, the epitomisation of the conflict between good and evil. Glenalvon was slain but not before he had mortally wounded Norval. Mrs Jackson brought to the fore the pathos of the mother grieving over her child's body:

> Hope and fear reigned alternately in her countenance, and when he died, her sudden falling as dead, fully expressed that the tide of sorrow, come to its height, had overwhelmed her powers. Her reviving was natural, and then frenzy possessed her whole frame. Her words thrilled through every ear, and her rapid exit, almost made the relation of Anna unnecessary, as some act of desparation could truly close the climax[24]

Lady Randolph leapt from the cliff-top to her death, an action which, preserving dramatic propriety, took place off stage. Mrs Siddons's interpretation similarly began in a low key and then rose to manic strength. Macready wrote that

> she had sunk in a state of insensibility on his body. On the approach of Randolph and Anna she began to recover recollection ... Leaning over [Young Norval], and gazing with despairing fondness on his face. She spoke out in her heartrending tones –
> My son! – My son!
> My beautiful, my brave! ...

The anguish of her soul seemed at length to have struck her brain. The silence of her fixed and vacant stare was terrible, broken at last by a loud and frantic laugh that made the hearers shudder. She then

R. Cruikshank, Del.

White, Sc.

Douglas.

Lady Randolph. Despair! despair!

Act V, Scene 1.

An engraving from a drawing made by Robert Cruikshank during a performance of *Douglas*; Lady Randolph sinks down in mourning over her slain son Young Norval. To the left of the drawing is a suggestion of a cut-wood. (*George Speaight*.)

sprang up, and, with a few self-questioning words indicating her purpose of self-destruction, hurried in the wild madness of desparation from the scene.[25]

The strength with which she played her last few lines and ran to the cliff-top was remarked on by Mrs Piozzi: 'I saw the exertions she made with some little anxiety'.[26] This did not detract from the greatness of Siddons's performance. G. F. Cooke described it as a 'sublime and attractive exhibition'.[27]

The usual reaction to the last act of the play was one of 'unfeigned tears' demonstrating, claimed David Hume, the command which the playwright had won 'over every affection of the human breast'.[28] He proceeded to make his well-known assertion that in the writings of Home was to be found 'the true theatric genius of Shakespeare and Otway, refined from the unhappy barbarism of the one and the licentiousness of the other'. Robert Burns expressed similar sentiments in his prologue for a benefit performance: 'Here *Douglas* forms wild Shakespeare into plan' ...[29] The opinions of both men were tersely summarised in the question shouted from the pit of the Canongate Theatre during the first season of the play: 'Weel, lads; what think you of Wully Shakespeare now?'[30]

Well into the nineteenth century *Douglas* was a stock piece in the repertoire of the provincial theatre as well as a stand-by for the private playhouse; it remained in the repertoire of the toy theatre until today. But even before Siddons had appeared in the revival of 1811 some had discovered that they could not suspend their disbelief in the prosy artificiality of Home's tragedy. The anonymous author of *The Miniature* (1806) satirised a production in a private theatre in which the wilds of Scotland were represented by a collection of hot-house plants; Lady Randolph was inaudible; Glenalvon was played by an innocuous Lord Foppington and the Young Norval, Master Marmozet, 'was decorated with every splendour that fashion could devise, and the simple plaid could hardly be distinguished through a profusion of jewels'.[31] When in 1856 William Makepeace Thackeray described a visit to the play, he viewed it with the eyes of a man jaundiced by a century of its stage history. Perhaps General Lambert's final words on Lady Randolph in *The Virginians* expressed an opinion felt by many of Thackeray's generation:

When Lady Randolph's friend described how her mistress had 'flown like lightning up the hill, and plunged herself into the empty air', Mr Lambert said he was delighted to be rid of her. 'And as for that story of her early marriage,' says he, 'I have my very strongest doubts about it.'[32]

The Castle Spectre by Matthew Gregory Lewis is a typical example of a gothic melodrama. An outline of the plot, giving a hint of the atmosphere of the piece as well as its contents, appeared in the *Monthly Mirror*:

> *Angela*, the heroine of the piece, is in love with *Earl Percy*, and is herself beloved by her uncle, *Earl Osmond*, who, in a family feud, has killed her mother, and who supposes himself to be the murderer of her father. But the life of *Reginald* has been preserved by an old servant, who, fearing fatal consequences to himself, keeps him somewhat inhumanly [*sic*], chained in a dungeon for 16 years. This *Earl Osmond* discovers in the progress of the piece, and endeavours in vain, to make her father's life the price of *Angela's* consent to his wishes. By missing her way, in her endeavours to escape, *Angela* stumbles upon her father; *Osmond* comes immediately after with his assassins; A GHOST follows close upon his heels; and after the ghost, in comes *Earl Percy* with his retainers. During the hesitation and fright occasioned by the apparition, *Angela* stabs her uncle, and after that heroic act, embraces *Percy* and *Reginald* with all the softness imaginable, and so concludes the CASTLE SPECTRE.[33]

Lewis set the plot in and beneath Conway Castle on the North Wales coast. The two principal characters, the Earl Osmond and Angela, were polarisations of virtue and wickedness and the resistance of that virtue to importuning lust formed the inner drama. From the start the audience must have realised that any deviation from the intrinsic nature of each of the principal characters was an impossibility; one's interest lay in watching the confrontations which arose from this gothic morality.

By 1797, the year of the play's first production, public taste had veered away from the Otrantoesque castle, with its gloom, mediaeval chivalry, spectres and unexplained mystery. Sheridan, then manager of Drury Lane, urged Lewis to 'confine [his] Ghost to the Greenroom' but perversely Lewis decided to introduce the appearance of Evelina's spirit on two occasions, making each of these a theatrical highlight.[34] The location was an inspired choice. Conway Castle had become part of the gothic consciousness. Both de Loutherbourg and Turner had drawn the attention of the public to it with its bastion strength, standing on an isolated promontory.[35] Lewis's play was in part responsible for ending that isolation, for tourists came to search out the ruin. Amongst them, in old age, was Mrs Siddons who sat at one of the glassless windows watching 'the river glowing in the balmy sunshine – the vessels gliding up and down – and the glorious Welsh mountains'.[36]

Lewis was fortunate in his cast. The lengthy role of Angela was taken by Dorothy Jordan, commended as 'the soul of the Performance' by a writer in the *Monthly Visitor*.[37] The heroine was the person with whom the audience identified and Michael Young's response to her was clearly stated: 'Angela is a being who clings round the heart, and seems to guide its sensations through the piece; for her sake you love Percy and detest Osmond'.[38] The part required great energy, so much so that Jordan felt unable to sing the song assigned to her in the fourth act and this was omitted in performance.[39] William Barrymore 'spiritedly' played the Earl Osmond and his 'tortures of guilt [were] well displayed', pronounced a critic.[40] The *True Briton* realised that his portrayal of guilt effectively stressed the moral aspect of the play.[41] The Spectre of the title was personated by Mrs Powell. John Philip Kemble essayed the part of the romantic hero, Percy. It was an unlikely role for him: he was tall, slowly spoken and statuesque. Presumably Kemble himself elected to take the part, although he disliked the play intensely.[42]

A distant view of Conway Castle, 'the most melancholy mansion' (1.1) Motley described it, came into sight as the curtain rose. Thomas Greenwood the Elder had designed the scenes but he died prior to the production leaving his son to supervise their completion.[43] The audience was drawn into the Castle Hall, a setting used a number of times. It was a complex structure with a continuous upper gallery and an open screen through which a long-vista was obtained, terminated by a tall gothic window: tawdry decorations, a few heraldic trophies, a tin helmet, a tabard and some banners, were hung on the set. The difficulty Greenwood had experienced was evident: he was designing for a play set in an indetermi-

'Conway Castle' by P J de Loutherbourg; one may conjecture how de Loutherbourg would have created a stage set from this painting which, especially in

the rocks and distant castle, appears to be conceived as a series of receding planes. (*National Maritime Museum.*)

nate mediaeval past. The 'Antiquary', whose remarks have
appeared before, attended the performance and was disappointed.
The scene, he claimed, was 'taken from the antient modes of the
Saxon and pointed arched works' but it did not 'accord with the
arrangments of our castellated structures'.[44]

Later in the play the audience saw a spacious hall containing
an arched and lofty window (2.3). It was onto the ledge of this
that Percy leapt to make his escape at the end of the scene. The
stage direction specified the functional furniture required in the
scene – a couch on one side of the stage and a table and chair
on the other. During the course of the action the chair was placed
on the table, making a series of levels by means of which Percy
could leap to freedom. Boaden described Kemble's galvanisation:

> ...he had to climb from a sofa to a Gothic window, and ... he has
> to fall from the height flat again at his length upon the said sofa, and
> seem asleep, as they had before seen him. This he did, as boldly and
> suddenly, as if he had been shot.[45]

The run up to the sill was repeated and, calling on angels to protect
him, the normally staid actor completed his leap through the
window.

Lewis used a range of interiors, one of which was the so-called
Cedar-room (3.3), backed by a pair of folding doors leading to
the oratory. Above this was another traceried window. Full length
portraits of *a Lady* and *a Warrior armed* formed two of the wings;
the first of these portraits slid to one side to reveal a secret passage.
The only furniture in the room was a bed. One is left in doubt
from the stage directions whether this room was the same as
Angela's Apartment (4.2) in the following act. If so, the setting
required another window through which Angela could gaze. Montague Summers suggests that Lewis, in his descriptions of the scenes,
had in mind the rooms of his childhood home at Stanstead Hall
in Essex.[46] Whether he mentioned this to Greenwood is not known.
However, the Cedar Room seemed a strange jumble of functional
pieces determined by the action, as the 'Antiquary' found:

> I have never read of a Cedar Room in our antient histories; nor do
> I believe that such a kind of room is among us at the present day.
> My eyes informed me that the whole scene appears as NEW work,

of an unaccountable mixture, of some of the features of our pointed arch mode of architecture, and that sort of architecture which owes its origin to the genius of the painter.[47]

At the second use of the scene Angela was discovered standing by a window through which the moon could be seen. The romantic lighting required was easily achieved by placing lamps in the wings and directing the light from these by means of baffles onto Angela's face. It was a touching effect and may have prompted John Keats to describe the window of Madeline's room, 'a casement high and triple arched', in 'The Eve of Saint Agnes'.[48] The quiet opening tableau gave way to dramatic revelations: Angela learnt not only of her mother's murder but also that her father lived in the dungeons beneath the castle. Osmond entered the apartment adventitiously brandishing the dagger with which Evelina had been slain sixteen years earlier. Overcome by the weight of his guilt Osmond fell senseless into the arms of his servants who carried him away. Having raised the key of the scene Lewis brought it to completion with his splendid set piece. A gentle lullaby sung to a guitar accompaniment marked the beginning of a transformation. As a bell started to toll, backlighting illuminated panels of stained glass (possibly coloured silks) set in doors in the back wall. These swung open and an illuminated oratory came into view.[49] One wonders whether part of the back-scene also opened in order to give an unimpeded vista into the chapel. In a Covent Garden prompt book for a revival of the play in 1825 the note occurs 'Doors open and flats off': two centre sections of the back-scene seem to have been removed.[50] The lighting focused the attention of the audience on to a tall, female figure in the oratory:

> ... *her white and flowing garments spotted with blood; her veil is thrown back, and discovers a pale and melancholy countenance; her eyes are lifted upwards, her arms extended towards heaven and a large wound appears on her bosom* (4.2).

To accompany the apparition Michael Kelly, the musical director for the production, selected a chaconne or slow dance by Niccolo Jommelli.[51] Boaden described the mime:

> ... the figure began slowly to advance; it was the spirit of Angela's mother, Mrs Powell, in all her beauty, with long sweeping envelopments

A scene from the author's production of *The Castle Spectre* at the Theatre Royal, Winchester; a confrontation between the Earl Osmund (Geoffrey Ridden) and Angela (Sue Evans). (*Photo: Peter Jacobs.*)

of muslin attached to the wrist ... Mrs Jordan *cowered* down motionless with terror, and Mrs Powell bent over her prostrate duty, in maternal benediction: in a few minutes she entered the oratory again, the doors closed, and darkness once more enveloped the heroine and the scene.[52]

The scene, theatrically effective, spoke more eloquently than Lewis's dialogue: '... it cannot be denied,' stated the *European Magazine*, 'that the silence and the gestures of the ghost operate very forcibly on the audience'.[53] In provincial theatres the scene was sometimes contrived by the use of a transparency, a saving on both space and cost.[54] In spite of the praise given to the overall effect of the scene, the Spectre's lack of speech prompted some spectators to compare her with Lord Burleigh, the silent, thinking actor of *The Critic*, an unjust stricture, for Lewis was bent on creating atmosphere as much as dialogue in this and later plays.[55]

An interlude in the Castle Hall divided the two scenes set in Angela's apartment. Here took place Osmond's nightmare, which gave the performer an opportunity to display his wild remorse for Evelina's murder. The horror of decay, much in evidence in Lewis's earlier work, *The Monk*, was expressed in Osmond's description of the rotting cadaver of the murdered woman:

'We meet again this night!' murmured her hollow voice! 'Now rush to my arms, but first see what you have made me! – Embrace me, my bridegroom! We must never part again!' – While speaking, her form withered away: the flesh fell from her bones; her eyes burst from their sockets: a skeleton, loathsome and meagre, clasped me in her mouldering arms! (4.1).[56]

How was such an overwrought episode to be played? In his work on stage gesture Henry Siddons singled out this incident as a challenge to the actor and suggested that he 'staggers, sinks into the arms of his attendants; and ought, when he recovers, to retreat from some object present to his mental eye, which inspires him with terror, and from which he is all anxiety to remove himself'.[57] Certainly the portrayal demanded great energy and it was at this juncture in the play that Graves Aickin, whilst performing at Cheltenham, collapsed and died from a burst blood-vessel.[58]

The fifth act took the audience into the dungeons of Conway Castle. An extant design for a dungeon by Greenwood the Elder corresponds to the requirements of the final scene of the play.[59]

(*left*) Matthew Gregory Lewis, playwright. (*Bodleian Library, Oxford (*39.1160*).*)

(*right*) Reginald (Ian Crowe), the prisoner of the dungeon, is threatened by Osmund; another episode from the Winchester production of *The Castle Spectre*. (*Photo; Peter Jacobs.*)

The drawing shows a vaulted semi-circular chamber, as vast as any Piranesi-designed prison, with a passageway disappearing into the wings and a doorway set high in the wall from which steps descend to the dungeon floor. It was a spacious building as, according to convention, the complete cast assembled in it at the conclusion. Immured here since his wife's death was Reginald, the rightful owner of Conway. Prisoners were expected to induce pity in their audiences but Lewis made Reginald pathetic to the point of humour:

> *Reginald, pale and emaciated, in coarse garments, his hair hanging wildly about his face, and a chain bound round his body, lies sleeping upon a bed of straw* (5.3).

The notched stick lying on the floor, the symbol of time spent, was reminiscent of the makeshift calendar of Laurence Sterne's prisoner in *The Sentimental Journey*, which was to be parodied in future writings such as *The Rovers*.[60] Lewis had ruminated on this prisoner for some time, drawing the subject from Goethe.[61]

124

The last moments of the play were filled with excitement and action: the entry of Osmond with his retinue, lusting for Angela and removing at a stroke the problems of consanguinity in his assertion, 'I have influence at Rome'; the news that Percy, to date so ineffective a hero, had surrounded the castle; Osmond's attempt to stab Reginald balanced by Angela's thwarted attempt, in turn, to stab her uncle. Despatches to the death were impeded by the sudden and last appearance of the Spectre accompanied by a 'tumult of applause'; she threw herself between the contending parties, eliciting shrieks and hysteria from the side boxes. 'We would seriously caution ladies in a certain way,' advised the *Monthly Visitor*, 'against seeing the representation of *The Castle Spectre*.'[62]

The strong impact of the play caused audiences to suspend judgement on it. Young's enthusiasm for the piece was typical of many:

> The long run which this play had the first season, the numerous times it has been performed since, the many editions it has gone through, and the power it still retains over the feelings of the audience, prove its merit beyond all praises which have, and can be, bestowed upon it.[63]

On reflection theatre-goers realised that, spectacular as much of the play had been, weaknesses were there. The Spectre came in for much criticism: she was a 'sham ghost', extraneous to the plot. Certainly she had atmospheric value, she 'made night hideous', but on the other hand she was employed too obviously as a claptrap.[64] Lord Byron summed up these opinions:

> Let Spectre-mongering Lewis aim, at most
> To course the Galleries, or to raise a ghost.[65]

Samuel Taylor Coleridge took an optimistic view of the piece, praising Lewis's management of the situations, in spite of the fact that many were borrowed and 'absolutely pantomimical'. Even the patchwork nature of the plagiarism could be excused, for Lewis sewed the pieces 'into an excellent whole'.[66]

On a pedantic level it seemed inevitable that the 'Antiquary' would write to the *Gentleman's Magazine* criticising the 'mediaeval' costumes. Two examples suggest the approximate nature of the designs. Osmond wore a 'habit' which was 'cut out from the several fashions of the last century'; around his neck was a 'modern-tied

125

handkerchief' edged with an unsuccessful imitation of a ruff.[67] Some
of Reginald's clothes were appropriate to the part of the prisoner
but he spoilt the effect by sporting a gracefully tied sash over
his shoulder. A surer test of the reaction of the audience to both
scenes and dresses is to be found in a brief remark of *The Times*
correspondent: respectively they were 'remarkably beautiful' and
'appropriate'.[68]

In 1799 the fortunes of Drury Lane were ailing and Richard
Brinsley Sheridan, attempting to create a production which would
act as a money-spinner, turned to the popular German writer,
August von Kotzebue, for the source of a play.[69] He selected *Die
Spanier in Peru* (1797). In this Kotzebue described the conquest
of the Peruvians by the Spanish conquistador, Pizarro, focusing
on the contrast between the cruelty of the Spanish catholics and
the gentle virtues of the native people. Such plot as the epic allowed
centred on the successful leadership of Rolla, the Peruvian hero,
in stemming the advancing foe.[70] A defector from the Spanish army,
Alonzo, by his marriage to a Peruvian woman, Cora, and in his
friendship for Rolla, served as a link with both nationalities in
the inevitable struggle.

The settings in Sheridan's adaptation of Kotzebue's play determined the gothic nature of *Pizarro*: there were the solitary places
made terrifying by thunderstorms in which the lonely figure of
Cora could hide; the Valley of the Torrent with its fragile bridge
spanning the ravine brought a familiar image to the stage; and
the dungeon, although translated to South America, had lost none
of its massive strength. Several of the characters, too, were
obviously based on stock gothic. Pizarro was a personification
of greed, applying force to satiate his appetite. What hope had
Cora against the insuperable odds confronting her? The pathetic
image she presented to her audience placed her firmly in the category of the gothic heroine.

Knowing no German, Sheridan based his drama on translations
made by Anne Plumptre, *The Spaniards in Peru*, Thomas Dutton,
Pizarro in Peru, and Matthew Lewis, *Rolla*.[71] Plumptre's work,
on which Sheridan principally relied, was a close, careful translation, totally lacking in dramatic vitality. In order to achieve success

Skelt's characters in *Pizarro*; in the vignette Rolla is seen with Cora's child on the bridge over the torrent whilst a Spanish soldier fires from the cliff-top. (*George Speaight.*)

it was important that Kemble and Siddons should appear. Sheridan conceived the part of Rolla for Kemble and he built the hero into an archetypal figure representing all stands made against advancing foes, a topical subject at the end of the eighteenth century as English forces mobilised in the southern counties to repel Napoleon's awaited attacks. Siddons was cast in the role of Elvira. Kotzebue made her a slattern, a trull lounging in the Spanish camp, selfishly entangling herself in Pizarro's affections. Sheridan, with Siddons in mind, was forced to heighten her moral qualities, giving her something of the dignity of a heroine. It was a role which depended on artifice and contrasted with Cora's natural simplicity. That ingenuous part was taken by Dorothy Jordan. Barrymore, who had previously given a forceful characterisation of the Earl Osmond, played the title role.

Settings and costumes were 'entirely new'.[72] All of the Drury

Lane scene-painters seem to have contributed to the settings: on
the bills appeared the names of Marinari, Greenwood, Demaria,
Banks and Blackmore with Johnston responsible for the machines.
The women's dresses were designed and made by Miss Rein and
the costumiers Underwood and Gay were also engaged. Another
pair of costumiers, Brooks and Heath, appear to have reproduced
the dresses as a speculation and these were hired or sold to provincial companies.[73] As well as performing, Kemble was responsible
for the direction of the piece and his prompt books for the production gave insights into the staging.[74]

A *magnificent Pavilion near Pizarro's Tent – a View of the Spanish
Camp in the back Ground* (1.1) was at first revealed – a more spectacular opening than the tent interior in which Plumptre set the corresponding scene. A rough drawing by John Henderson Grieve
of Greenwood's design was described as depicting the interior of
the tent, although it is obviously the pavilion of Sheridan's directions.[75] It indicates a large archway set down-stage, flanked by
draped curtains, beyond which is a semi-circular colonnade backed
by more curtains, partly drawn, allowing the Spanish camp to be
seen in the distance. Skelt's toy theatre sheets gave an alternative.[76]
The exterior of Pizarro's tent was shown – a gaily curtained erection
with drapes drawn up into swags. The splendour of Greenwood's
scene, 'equal in point of brilliant effect to the best scenes of any
of our theatres' proclaimed *The Times*, captivated the audience.[77]

The scene changed to a *Bank surrounded by a wild Wood and
Rocks* (2.1), presumably a carpenter's scene set well down-stage
and consisting of little more than a painted landscape with a couple
of ground rows to suggest the rocks along the river-bank. The
wildness of the terrain may have given the audience a premonition
that Cora and her child, who featured in the episode, could become
involved in danger. In this scene Kemble's Rolla appeared wearing
a knee-length, white cotton tunic with a leopard skin toga-like
over his shoulder. Crossed leather thongs completed the picture
of simplicity. Young, who played the role after Kemble, wore the
same garb thus fixing the iconography, both on stage and in illustrations for the portrayal of the Inca hero.[78]

In the ten-minute playing time of this scene the Temple of the
Sun was set in position further upstage and, as the orchestra played

Drawings of Pizarro's pavilion and the Temple of the Sun on the reverse of a watercolour by John Henderson Grieve. (*Print Room, British Museum.*)

one of Michael Kelly's marches, the landscape parted revealing Gaetano Marinari's design. The Grieve sketch indicates that eight large columns supported the vaulting, which was probably in position from the start of the play and further pilasters formed a semi-circular apse. At the centre stood the altar situated, according to the prompt-book although not so shown in the drawing, at the top of a flight of steps. In the farthest position up-stage was the icon of the Sun God, 'transparent' as Grieve had noted and the focal point of the design. Gold foil was used in the decoration, a useful reflector of light adding lustre to the spectacle.

In the temple Rolla made an impassioned address to the Inca warriors, calling on them to defend their homeland. In reality this was an English politician's exhortation to patriotic endeavour, for it contained phrases which Sheridan himself had used in the House of Commons in support of George III's call for readiness against a French invasion.[79] A strong metrical beat helped to make the speech more impassioned; indeed, throughout this tragedy written in prose ('I cannot seriously approve of an heroic tragedy in prose,' wrote Hester Piozzi to Penelope Pennington)[80] Sheridan frequently embedded iambic feet into the dialogue:

> THEY by a strange frenzy driven, fight for power, for plunder, and extended rule – WE for our country, our altars and our homes. THEY follow an adventurer whom they fear – and obey a power which they hate – WE serve a Monarch whom we love – a God whom we adore (2.2).

Kemble was notorious for breaking lines with his terraced dynamics and over-wrought vocal colouring. The *Enchiridion Clericum* gave an amusing account of his delivery of the speech:

> Then mark the contrast when he comes to show
> God's majesty by voice depressed and low.
> Ourselves! as full and loud as he can bawl: –
> Our God – distinguished by a mighty fall.
> Observe you next how horror is exprest
> With tremulous accent and a tone deprest.[81]

When Young took over the part he too 'in a low key pronounced with slow solemnity the name of the Almighty', a continuing tradition not lost on the audience.[82] A procession of the Priests and

Virgins of the Sun made its way from the rear of the stage and
grouped on either side of the altar as the orchestra played a march
by Christoph Gluck.[83] To mark the completion of the ritual, fire
from above lit up the altar. Suddenly the ordered ceremonial was
shattered by news of the enemy approaching. Cora sped with her
child to a remote sanctuary as the Inca soldiers prepared for war.

A two-minute carpenters' scene followed showing a woodland
glade which gave way to a *View of the Peruvian Camp* (2.4), possibly
another painted scene set immediately behind the former. Rejoicing
and sorrow marked the progress of the action: Rolla, shedding
fire with his sword, routed the enemy but Alonzo, fighting on behalf
of the Incas, was taken prisoner by the Spaniards.

A wild Retreat among stupendous Rocks (3.1), 'as tawdry as gilt
gingerbread', wrote Thomas Dutton, consisted in Skelt's version
of the scene of a wild English landscape, reminiscent of Dovedale,
in which a cavern was set.[84] The scene repeated, from the view-point
of the Peruvian women, the emotions which the soldiers had
expressed in the previous. A wood, set in the first grooves, formed
the next scene.[85] Pizarro's tent revealed in turn a *Dungeon in the
Rock* (4.1) set in position during the two previous scenes. The dungeon was based on a semi-circular construction viewed through
a foreground arch. The text required a recess at the back of the
prison and this took the form of a cavern.[86] Dutton commented
on the unsuitability of so grand a construction in a land in which
the Spaniards held but a fleeting foothold:

> Among other gross instances of incongruity in the *scenery* of this *panto-
> mimic* tragedy, we have to notice the introduction of a *magnificent*
> dungeon, built, *secundum artem*, with all its horrific appendages of
> bolts, bars, staples, massy pillars, subterraneous passages, etc.[87]

Almost lost in the cavernous space, Alonzo lay chained asleep,
until woken by Rolla who had terrorised the guard into allowing
him to penetrate the prison. He had arrived shrouded in a friar's
habit, bringing with him a well-used dramatic device: Alonzo and
Rolla would change costumes and places.

Two less elaborate scenes followed which, one gains the impression, were placed down-stage in order that the last of the set-pieces,
the Valley of the Torrent, could be prepared. The first scene showed

the interior of Pizarro's tent. Within, Pizarro realised that he had lost his hold on Elvira and she, as one of the truth figures of the play, harangued him on his selfish cruelty.[88] Pizarro crumbled not only before her but also before Rolla whom uncharacteristically he released with a statement which momentarily revealed his lost nobility: 'I cannot but admire thee, Rolla: I wou'd we might be friends' (4.2). The following scene, a dense forest beset by a violent thunderstorm, showed in the background a hermit's hut almost covered by boughs. Impetus was given to the plot by the theft of Cora's child by two Spanish soldiers. As she and Alonzo sought for the missing baby, his remark, 'See yonder hut among the trees' (5.1), was made ridiculous as the shack was set so far to the front it was in full view of the audience. '... one would suppose,' wrote Dutton, whose remarks about the production tended to be waspish, 'Cora must have been more intoxicated than the Spanish soldiers in the preceding scene not to notice it.'[89] The guards mentioned, according to the text, merely attended on Pizarro; the drunkenness was an example of actors' licence. When the scenes and the too-prominent hut were removed the Valley of the Torrent came into view, a wild and rocky location in which a cascade of water was surmounted by a bridge made from a felled tree. Instantly the audience must have realised that the precariousness of the bridge suggested a tragedy was about to occur. An impression of the stage arrangement can be gained from an engraving showing a revival of the play at Covent Garden in 1804.[90] On the back scene a sky-scape and distant mountains were painted. Wing pieces formed the rocky precipice with its picturesque gnarled trees growing between the boulders, giving way downstage to a framework of co-existent oaks and palms. A spacious area between the pro-scenium arch and the wing pieces, leaving the deck of the stage much in evidence, allowed plenty of room both for the principal characters and for the supernumeraries who marched onto the stage.

At the start of the scene the recaptured Rolla was brought in. The taunts a soldier hurled at his prisoner were interrupted by the arrival of further soldiers with Cora's child. Countering Pizarro's threats to keep the child from his mother, Rolla seized the infant, ran from the stage with him and reappeared on the

The Royal Family at Covent Garden Theatre.

Published Aug.ᵗ 1ˢᵗ 1804 by Richard Phillips 71 S.ᵗ Paul's Church Yard.

James Fittler's engraving of the Royal Family at a performance of *Pizarro* at the Theatre Royal, Covent Garden, in 1804 to mark the supposed recovery of George III from illness. Rolla snatches Cora's child from the Spanish soldiers prior to scaling the rock face. (*Author's Collection.*)

straddling tree-trunk, a vulnerable target. He tore the tree from its base and, injured, escaped with the child. Kemble's performance at this juncture was electrifying. As he seized the baby he hoisted him aloft on his left arm and then, with dagger drawn, struck an attitude for the single line: 'Who moves one step to follow me, dies upon the spot' (5.2). In this heroic pose Sir Thomas Lawrence painted the actor and subsequently Young adopted the same attitude.[91] What followed was described by Boaden:

> The herculean effort of his strength – his passing the bridge – his preservation of the infant, though himself mortally wounded, excited a sensation of alarm and agony beyond anything perhaps that the stage has exhibited.[92]

It has to be admitted, however, that in spite of this suggested

(*left*) An engraving from Sir Thomas Lawrence's painting of Rolla (modelled by Jackson the Puguilist based on John Philip Kemble's attitude) at the moment of retrieving Cora's baby; this pose passed into the iconography of the play and was employed by Edmund Kean in his revival of *Pizarro*. (*Theatre Collection, University of Bristol.*)

(*right*) Ataliba (Michael Roberts) sends out his troops to battle with the invading Spaniards; a shot from the author's production of *Pizarro* at the Arts Centre, King Alfred's College, Winchester. (*Photo: Peter Jacobs.*)

nobility the rescue of the child was, according to Oulton, 'generally attended by laughter'.[93] Possibly the audience found difficulty in suspending its disbelief and saw no more than an asthmatic actor hoisting aloft one of the property dolls.

The two final scenes formed a coda. Sheridan's stage direction required *Ataliba's tent* (5.3), for which Kemble substituted 'A Landscape', setting it in the first grooves. On the floor the stagehands laid a green carpet and the audience realised, before the action took place, that Rolla's wound was mortal.[94] His last moments were spent in restoring the child to Cora. *A romantic part of the Recess amongst the Rocks* (5.4) followed, in which 'Cut Woods' were used. The stipulated romanticism of the setting was at variance

134

with the clamour of the Peruvians as they drove the Spaniards from the field. The hour of retribution struck: Alonzo slayed the Spanish tyrant. Kemble added a further scene change, unstipulated by Sheridan, possibly a return to the Valley of the Torrent, for the solemnity of Rolla's funeral:

> *A Solemn March* ['Dead March' according to Kelly] – *Procession of Peruvian Soldiers, bearing Rolla's Body on a Bier, surrounded by Military Trophies – In the looks of the King and of all present, the Triumph of the Day is lost, in mourning for the fallen Hero* (5.4).[95]

On this sad tableau the green curtain slowly descended.

Problems arose with the smooth manipulation of the many scene changes. The theatre was closed immediately prior to the run for mechanical practice sessions and for Kemble to drill the crowd scenes. On the first night more than one hiatus arose, especially with the unhitching of the bridge over the Valley of the Torrent and the management debated whether to cancel the Saturday performance in order to work further on the mechanics of the show. However the schedule was maintained and by the fourth performance the production ran smoothly. This was an achievement as, after the inordinate five hour length of the first night, Sheridan made severe cuts in the text which reduced the intervening time between each scene change.[96]

As a spectacle the play was acclaimed on all sides: painters, machinists and carpenters had reached a zenith of success.[97] Whilst the audience was in the theatre it responded warmly to Sheridan's contribution to the evening but in the cool light of the following day some of its members may have inclined to Percy Fitzgerald's view that here was just the sort of tragedy which Sheridan twenty years earlier had ridiculed in *The Critic*: an evening of bombastic dialogue and empty show.[98] William Gifford highlighted the purists' feelings about such a use of spectacle:

> ... if you take from the German dramas their ... minute and ridiculous stage-directions, which seem calculated to turn the whole into a pantomime, nothing will remain but a *caput mortuum* ...[99]

The *Anti-Jacobin Review*, a Tory paper and no friend to Sheridan, faulted the tendency of German playwrights and their English adap-

Richard Sheridan as Pizarro riding triumphantly on the head of Rolla; as Sheridan had hoped, Pizarro was most successful at the Drury Lane box-office. (*Theatre Collection, University of Bristol.*)

tors to limit virtue to the lower classes or unsophisticated native peoples:

> In Pizarro we have a chief, or general, painted in the most infamous characters, being only meant as a malevolent portrait of men in high stations, although it is disguised with the cloak of history.[100]

The concentration in the last two scenes of the play on the death of Rolla, by which Sheridan skewed the focus away from the villain of the title role to the heroics of the Peruvian leader, seemed to some a superfluous statement. Dutton suggested Sheridan's principle was:

> ... that to render a tragedy truly *tragic*, it is indispensibly necessary to *murder* not only the principal *Dramatis Personae*, but the Tragedy itself.[101]

As with most of the gothic dramas, however, the merit of the piece lay in its theatrical impact. It was, and still is, a play in which the emotions of the audience can be stirred: the exotic foreign location, the progression of scenes, the mounting excitement of each of the rapidly composed situations, the forceful simplification of good working to thwart evil and the unambiguous statement of the final tragedy all contributed towards the entertainment. At root it was as entertainment that gothic drama was acceptable, not as a literary text nor as the distillation of a philosophical idea.

The plays in these three case studies reflect the changes which occurred from the middle to the end of the eighteenth century in the development of the gothic drama. Home's play, *Douglas*, was an essay in reserved presentation: the strong influence of classical Greek tragedy was reflected in its structure and dramatic propriety, restraints which were absent in Lewis's *The Castle Spectre* and Sheridan's *Pizarro*. The former was a rambling pantomime, reminiscent of a ballad in its hankering after a world of 'faerie' summed up in its castle and its ghost — the two motifs which Lewis introduced into the title. *Pizarro* boasted an epic quality, with its exotic South American setting and its rousing tale of native chivalry and patriotism. *Douglas*, in spite of its title, was the first of a sprinkling of matriarchal tragedies. By the time *The Castle Spectre* was written the grieving matron had been banished to an aetherialised state; true, she re-appeared embodied in Cora but this was within the stock type of the youthful heroine. The villain, melodramatic in *The Castle Spectre* and disintegrative in *Pizarro*, was commanding the centre of the stage by the end of the 1790s. Sublimity was achieved not by a spectacle of pathos but by his energetic personification of lust and greed.

Spectacle played no part in *Douglas* but it was an essential element of the two later shows. Greenwood provided for Lewis a series of castle interiors, below and above ground, architecturally inept but not without grandeur. At the centre of the spectacle, like a jewel glowing in its casket, was the candle-lit oratory made mysterious by Evelina's ghost. Unstinting on expenditure, Sheridan organised the painters of Drury Lane to create for him a multiplicity of scenes, all tinsel and gold foil, rather than those examples of verisimilitude which de Loutherbourg would have brought to a series of geographical locations. It was a missed opportunity. Nevertheless, *Pizarro* illustrated the rising importance of spectacle by the end of the century.

The development of the dialogue ran parallel with that of the setting. With the exception of Glenalvon's register of villainy, the characters in *Douglas* spoke in an economical, dignified and simple blank verse, consonant with the restraint running through the play. In spite of its high bombast, the prose of *The Castle Spectre* stood the test of sixty years of regular revival; within the compass of this melodrama it works well. Rhetoric and political oratory, sentimental locution and sententious moralising formed a strange language compound in *Pizarro*. However, that the play soon faded from the stage is due instead to the cost of mounting it; it was the developing taste for changing spectacle – animal dramas were being given pride of place by the time the Spanish general was laid to rest – and not the dialogue which hustled the play out of the theatre.

Contrasted with these changes there were signs of constancy in the three plays. Most obvious was the appearance of the gothic paraphernalia. The castle figured in both Home's and Lewis's plays and, translated to South America, it took the form of Pizarro's pavilion and the dungeon into which Alonzo was flung. In each play the locations were remote, unvisited by most members of the audience and thereby viewed through a mist of singularity. A recapitulation of sad history and an impression of impending danger haunted the early lines of *Douglas* and *The Castle Spectre*; for Sheridan the future exploits of the Spaniards were more important than the past, although even he did not neglect to give retrospective hints of the noble qualities in Pizarro's earlier life. Theatre-goers present at *Douglas* would recognise in the two later plays the stock nature of the characters, an encapsulation in typification which required performers in all three dramas to break into high theatricality to give life to the roles. Many of the signals employed by the *fin-de-siecle* actor would be recognisable enough to draw a response from the *Douglas* audience. Development there had been but the basics remained.

Chapter Seven: The Response to the Gothic Drama

Sir Walter Scott, writing of his visits to the theatres of his childhood, remembered the magical hinterland which lay beyond the rising curtain; it was a landscape of

> woods and mountains and lakes, lighted, it seems to us, by another sun, and inhabited by a race of beings different from ourselves, whose language is poetry, whose dress, demeanour and sentiments seem something supernatural, and whose whole actions and discourses are calculated not for the ordinary tone of everyday life, but to excite the stronger and more powerful faculties . . .[1]

With maturity the magical impact became muted but new windows were opened as the visitor enjoyed

> the more sober pleasure of becoming acquainted with the higher energies of human passion, the recondite intricacies and complications of human temper and disposition, by seeing them illustrated in the most vivid manner by those whose profession it is to give life, form and substance to the creation of genius.[2]

So often in the gothic drama temper and disposition were simplistically portrayed as a moral conflict between good and evil: the hero became the representative of virtue which eventually triumphed; the heroine, a model of moral rectitude, was the petrified protagonist and the villain, the summation of scheming greed, was her effective antagonist. Performers breathed life into these too-familiar frameworks by their technical expertise and also by their own

139

emotional involvement in the well-tested situations of the plot. For their part, the members of the audience would respond to the hero, heroine and villain with an overtness that merged the life of auditorium and stage into a single organism as the play progressed. The role seems to have been of greater interest than the situations or the dialogue and so the audience's response to the stock characters conveniently forms a frame for our initial considerations.

Were the actions of the hero applauded, or was the approbation, which might have been afforded him given instead to the performer? As now the performer, rather than the role created by the playwright, received the ovation. A packed house had arrived to view Betty in the role of Achmet-Selim (*Barbarossa*, John Brown, 1754). In spite of the discomforts of overcrowding, complete quietness descended on the auditorium – 'not even a whisper could be heard', reported Boaden – in preparation for the young prodigy's entry.[3] He walked on to the stage and took his bow.

> Upon the thunder of applause that ensued, he was not '*much* moved'
> – he bowed very respectfully, but with amazing self-possession in a
> few moments turned him to his work . . .[4]

Today it is difficult to envisage how this child could perform the principal role surrounded by adult actors as the incongruity would remove any credibility from the performance. Yet Betty was accepted in the part. His own presentation must have been viewed in isolation from that of the others and evaluated on points of style; lack of maturity would have mattered little. There seems to be a parallel here with the easy allowance that was made for a discrepancy in age when Barry played Norval.

Panache and bravado were requisites of the hero's stage image, and the actor's competence in using the dialogue to combine his own personality with his stage persona would win delighted applause. Robert William Elliston, taking the part of Vivaldi in his own play, *The Venetian Outlaw* (1805), concluded his final speech with the line, 'I will not be interrogated! conduct me instantly to death!' (3.1) and gained immediately three successive rounds of applause.[5] How these were maintained is a mystery. Sometimes the quality the actor brought to the role was as effervescent as charm but yet this could win the audience's applause. The sight of Michael Kelly as Lord William (*The Haunted Tower*) stalking sword in hand along the castle battlements, a piece of swashbuckling which contrasted with the 'dignified and interesting' fashion that had marked his previous actions, nevertheless drew an enthusiastic response.[6] 'In a popular piece a great actor holding a sword in his left hand and making awkward passes with it, charms the audience,' commented Hannah Cowley, 'and brings down such applause as the bewitching Farquhar pants for in vain.'[7] In Kelly's flourishes there was a further hint at a clap-trap and delightedly the audience responded to the actor rather than to the established character.

In contrast, the plight of the heroine offered her presenter few opportunities to bring much of her own personality to the role, for she was straight-jacketed into a personation of extreme plight. The pathos rather than the performer gained the applause. Fanny Kelly in the role of Ellen (*The Falls of Clyde*) subjugated her character to a cloud of 'depression and melancholy, which was evidently the result of settled woe', wrote the critic of the *Theatrical Inquisitor*, commending the effect she had on her audience.[8] However, silent suffering was rare. The heroine's role usually demanded the spirited shrieks and sobs which Mrs Johnstone effected in her portrayal of Matilda (*Edgar*).[9] Confronted with the news that her brother would die unless she married the villainous Malcolm, the stage directions and the dialogue suggest the external force with which the misery involved was projected:

(*Matilda shrieks, and throws herself on her mother's neck.*)
Countess: O, my child!
Fly not to this sad bosom for relief.
Matilda: Where shall I find it else?
Oh horror! horror!
Edgar: How shall I speak of comfort
Who need so much? – (*aside*) – O yield not to despair!
Perhaps he will relent!
Matilda: Relent! – who! – what! – Malcolm?

Such a strength of projection must have been in Richard Payne Knight's mind when he contrasted the muted quality of pathos in everyday life with the 'display of vigour' necessary on the stage.[10] Only thus could the actress raise her condition to a sublime state. Unfortunate the woman who lacked the vocal power or stamina to project pathos so forcibly; the condemnation of a critic in *The Times* would apply to her too: 'The heroine . . . is beyond the powers of Miss de Camp'.[11] Obviously, the playwright may ill-serve the actress. Sophia Lee had undercut the impact of Sarah Siddons in *Almeyda* by anticipating news which eventually should have produced both suspense and pathos. In spite of the considerable vocal powers of Siddons 'the heroine's distress excited no compassion'.[12] Audiences responded to the subtleties of pointing and emphasis as well as to emotional batterings. Carl Philipp Moritz described the alacrity with which an audience would pick up the presentation of a 'single solitary sentiment' offering a 'singularly pathetic stroke', be it even as brief as the celebrated enquiry of Lady Randolph (*Douglas*), 'Was he alive?' (3.1).[13] As early as 1773 Oliver Goldsmith had remarked that sentimental drama needed only a heroine with a title and a 'mighty good heart to turn the ladies of the audience to tears'.[14] In that respect the drama of sentiment corresponded to the gothic. English patrons brought a sharpened sensibility to the playhouse which, as the remarks of various German visitors has indicated, other nationalities sometimes lacked. That tender weeping which accompanied Euphrasia's ill-considered thrust of the dagger into the tyrant's bosom in *The Grecian Daughter*, was replaced in New York by unseemly enthusiastic shouts.[15] English heroines were created for English audiences.

On the heroine the audience expended pity; the eventual downfall of the villain aroused the emotion of terror in the audience. Wickedness could meet its end in self-destruction. Whilst satisfaction was to be found in the sight of the termination of evil, could self-immolation be either satisfactory or moral? When he lived at the height of his powers, the energy with which the villain pursued his desires could arouse admiration and raise the spectator to feelings of sublimity, a paradox noted by Payne Knight.[16] Terror was a by-product of this sublime situation. Before the conclusion of *The Mysterious Husband* (Richard Cumberland, 1783) the villain, Davenant, poisoned but still alive, stabbed himself in front of the audience. In his dying speech he sought to excuse himself:

142

I am sorry to present a spectacle so bloody to you both: but poison
work'd too sluggishly, nor could I bear its agonies (5.1).

A favourable reception bore witness to the terror engendered by
his death.[17] The end of villainy justified the means whereby it was
achieved. Mistakenly playwrights could attempt to make horror
an end in itself and when this occurred protests were made. Bertie
Greatheed multiplied gruesome situations in the final act of *The
Regent* (1788): the audience witnessed Dianora's attempts to slay
Manuel, his retaliation in stabbing her, the villain's dying vision
of hell and the imminent decapitation of Carlos as he was held
over the block. This last action went too far and, in protesting
against the horrors, Mrs Thrale seemed to speak for the audience
as a whole.[18] In spite of objections, though, playwrights were
unabated in their use of violence over the following thirty years.
In 1816 Maturin, in presenting *Bertram* to the public, created a
violent last act to the play in which Bertram was discovered living
in the same room as the corpse of St Aldobrand whose murder
he had engineered. To intensify the villain's plight the world was
scaled down to a single chamber:

> I deemed that when I struck the final blow,
> Mankind expired, and we were left alone,
> The corse and I were left alone together
> The only tenants of a blasted world (5.2).

A writer found the situation difficult to stomach as it was more
than sufficient for those 'who have ever "supped their full of horrors"'.[19] Could not pity for the unfortunate man, pleaded the critic,
occasionally replace the horror?

When the gothic drama was cast in the mould of a morality
or a melodrama the emotional variant proposed by the question
was inconceivable. However the audiences did respond approvingly
to the emergence of the villain-hero, a character such as De Monfort, who lacked that singleness of purpose possessed by the old-
style villain but produced, in his divided response to the demands
of good and evil, a poetic and highly dramatic character, tinged
with a nobility in which lustres of the sublime gleamed. When
this type of villain reformed he brought an ineffective and, it must
be admitted, disappointing end to the play. The final speech of

the King of Naples in *Evadne* showed this weakness.[20] Redeemed by the heroine's virtue, he lamely claimed:

> Thou hast wrought
> A miracle upon thy prince's heart,
> And lifted up a vestal lamp, to show
> My soul its own deformity – my guilt! (5.1).

Drawing a stronger response from the audience was that villain-hero whose undoing and eventual death was caused by his own actions, in which lay the implication that any judgement on him was a self-condemnation, rather than retribution inflicted externally by an accident of the natural world. The audience admired the villain-hero and to a point identified with him. This tended to elevate the worth of gothic tragedy and its heightened effect on the audience may be summarised in William Hazlitt's words: the tragedy resolved the pain and suffering of the central figure 'into the sense of power by the aid of imagination and by grandeur of conception and character'.[21]

Information about the audience's response to the actors' presentation of the principal roles must be balanced by its response to the play as a whole. Of course, an appreciation of a successful role portrayal could be extrapolated from an unsuccessful play. A voice from the gallery on the first night of *Julian and Agnes* described it as an 'ill-made pudding' which was blessed with 'one plumb and two currants in it', the performances of Kemble, Siddons and Anne Biggs.[22] These performers were praised but the play was dismissed:

> ... the audience soon grew *drowsy*, and passed by a natural transition from *yawning* to *coughing*, and from *coughing* by a transition equally natural, to the *dernier resort* of groaning and hissing.[23]

'Not successful', wrote Kemble in his notebook.[24] Occasionally literary evaluations, judgements on the plays from 'within the closet', were made and these, with changing criteria, appear ridiculous today: that the works of John Home represented Shakespeare perfected, or that Robert Jephson's dialogue could rival that of John Dryden were evaluations fettered by the academic acceptances of the eighteenth-century reader.[25] In order to be justly evaluated the gothic drama had to be witnessed in the theatre, for soon after such seminal productions as *Douglas* and *The Grecian Daughter* it had established itself as a form of spectacle. In today's theatre responses and their expression have changed, leaving us to question whether terror in watching Ordonio rant his way through *Remorse* could have been experienced, or pity felt for the plight of Angela in *The Castle Spectre* in which she was no more than a pasteboard representation of virtue. Yet, as has been shown already, a variety of writers claimed that the performers drew enthusiastic and sometimes voluble responses from their audiences. Such reactions can only be viewed within the framework of the period. For the Georgian theatregoer the successful gothic drama was one which theatrically exploited locations, dialogue and spectacle. There was little that was new in the incidents of the plot. A few stock situations were used with such repetition that accusations of plagiarism were frequently made.[26] Locations, however, set the emotional tone of the piece. In the later gothic dramas they also introduced audiences, however naïvely, to countries as yet unvisited by most Englishmen. The impact of a range of specific locations was due in part to their common use by playwrights, novelists, poets and painters. Dialogue was often bombastic and innocent of psychological motivation; yet a performer by his dynamism, technical expertise and emotional involvement could invest it with an excitement thrilling to hear. In retrospect, the growth of spectacle on the stage might indicate that the audience found the content of the dramas wanting and occasionally, as in the equestrian interludes of *Blue-Beard*, spectacle was merely an overlay supplied by the acting-manager. Yet in such successes as *Valentine and Orson*, *The Falls of Clyde* and *The Miller and His Men* spectacle was an integral part of the plot, advancing the narrative and enhancing the subtext with symbolism.

There was, however, more to gothic drama than an escape from reality into mediaevalism and spectacle. It could present to audiences the moral and subconscious worlds. The moral world of the gothic drama was self-evident in the personification of virtue and wickedness, whether the conflict took place between the villain and the hero, or within the heart of one man. Less overtly the gothic reflected the subconscious aspirations and fears of some members of the audience. The Industrial and the French Revolutions brought respectively unrest and horror in their wake and this was reflected in the turbulence of the gothic dramas; the constant travels of the stage characters were a mirroring of the ingress of the artisan class to urban areas and the rootlessness which inadequate living conditions induced. This was an age when various strata of society were harassed and repressed – by debt-collectors, by the squirarchy, by excisemen, by employers – and these powers were expressed on stage in various punitive guises, – the inquisition, the autocrat, prison, the banditti, rampaging orders of monks. This undercurrent gave veracity and a subconscious realism to plays which appeared to move in a realm of escapist fantasy. Such factors as these sharpened the awareness of audiences, influencing their evaluations of plays.

After 1820 the gothic drama tended to dwindle at the patent houses and the remaining spasmodic entertainments of the genre were given in such theatres as the Olympic, the Royal Coburg and the Lyceum. Here the established role representatives moved from the confines of castle and convent to the manor house and the rustic cottage. A social battle was fought between the rapacious squire and the dispossessed cottager in place of the moral struggle formerly witnessed. Landscapes gave way to the endless tunnelled streets of the city, in which the hero was confronted by squalor, poverty and temptation. A new threat in the form of alcohol replaced the terrors of the scowling villain. The ethos which had shaped the earlier gothic dramas was lost.

Nevertheless the gothic tradition is not dead. It continues in both novels and films and occasionally appears on the stage. Two works, both relying on the tradition of horror fragments rather than on the inheritance of the tale of terror, contribute to current explorations of the phenomenon. In 1818, immediately prior to the conclusion of the period under investigation, Mary Shelley wrote *Frankenstein*. This has given a resurgence to theatrical gothic in *The Rocky Horror Show*, an entertainment which since its first presentation thirty years ago has drawn a cult following and provokes a highly active audience participation uniting both performers and spectators. Interestingly, a later film version disseminated through video has given enthusiasts an opportunity to memorise the dialogue so that during live performances many of the audience eagerly and audibly anticipate the highlights of the show. In this respect they resemble an eighteenth-century audience watching a repertoire favourite such as *Douglas*.

The other novel is *Dracula*, written by Bram Stoker in 1897. Stoker, Henry Irving's secretary, possessed a strong sense of theatre, evident in the easy translation of his ideas to film in *Nosferatu*, of which both an early black and white version (1922) and, as a self-conscious tribute, a remake in colour (1979), introduce the tragic narrative to new generations.

The gothic novel is still able to command respect. An example is Iris Murdoch's work, *The Bell*, set in the remote house of Imber surrounded by barely tamed gardens and woodland.[27] A group of life's jetsam shelter within its walls, welding themselves into a community, a reflection of the close-knit existence of eighteenth-century banditti who felt themselves to be society's outcasts. Occasionally the submerged bell of the title is heard reminding the residents of the paranormal world. The reiterated use of the landscape to mirror the changing moods of the novel's key personalities securely places *The Bell* within the same terrain as Ann Radcliffe's writing.

Cinema and television directors have fastened on to the gothic to a greater degree than novelists. A class of budget film harks back to the genre but the overstatements of some directors trespass beyond the confines of terror, indulging in scenes which provoke horror. Indeed, 'horror-movie' becomes an accepted term and the films present a debased version of the root from which they have grown. Repugnance was not a reaction Georgian gothic writers strove to achieve. However, many other directors have discovered that the gothic tradition is a gift to the visual media: photographed from the air the vastness of the landscape is laid open; decaying houses retain their unseen terrors; screen music continues to give commentary on the emotions of the characters portrayed; the sound of the cascade can create unease even if it has been recast as a gushing shower in Alfred Hitchcock's *Psycho*. In today's acceptance of these motifs there is a transcendence of time and culture. Terror and pity still sleep in the human heart; they wait to be aroused.

Notes and References

CHAPTER ONE: THE GOTHIC SPIRIT

1. *St James' Chronicle*, 16–19 December 1797; *Morning Chronicle*, 21 January 1797.
2. *Monthly Mirror*, IV (December 1797), 357.
3. Samuel Johnson, *A Dictionary of the English Language* (1775).
4. Miles Peter Andrews, *The Songs, Recitatives, Airs, Duets, Trios and Choruses introduced into the Pantomime Entertainment of 'The Enchanted Castle'* (1786), p. iv.
5. An extended discussion on the gothic territory may be found in: David Jarett, '"Gothic" as a term in Literary Criticism in the Eighteenth Century', unpublished thesis, University of Oxford, 1968; Alfred Longueil, 'The Word "Gothic" in Eighteenth Century Criticism', *Modern Language Notes*, XXXVIII (1923), 453–60; Devendra P. Varma, *The Gothic Flame* (1957).
6. Horace Walpole, *The Castle of Otranto* (1764), ed. Wilmarth Sheldon Lewis (1969). An evaluation of his contribution to the gothic genre is to be found in Varma, *Gothic Flame*, pp. 44–65.
7. Horace Walpole, *The Yale Edition of Horace Walpole's Correspondence*, ed. Wilmarth Sheldon Lewis (1937–80), X, 307.
8. Walpole, *Otranto*, ed. Lewis, p.22. Warren Hunting Smith contrasted the two buildings in 'Strawberry Hill and *Otranto*', *The Times Literary Supplement*, 23 May 1936. Walpole's eclectic taste and scholarship are explored in: Charles Locke Eastlake, *A History of the Gothic Revival* (1872), pp. 44–51.
9. John Aikin and Anna Letitia Barbauld, *Miscellaneous Pieces in Prose* (1792), p. 121 and pp. 127 ff.
10. S. M. Ellis, *The Life of Michael Kelly* (1930), p. 254.
11. Ann Radcliffe, *The Mysteries of Udolpho* (1794), ed. Bonamy Dobrée (Oxford, 1980), p. 30; see also pp. 78, 102, 227, 230, 302, 358 and 631.

12. Horace Walpole, *Letters of Horace Walpole*, ed. Mrs Paget Toynbee (Oxford, 1903–05), VI, 195; Walpole, *Otranto*, ed. Lewis, p. 3.
13. Clara Reeve, *The Old English Baron* (1777), Preface to the Second Edition (1778), ed. James Trainer (1967), p. 3.
14. *Critical Review*, LXVI (1788), 359. A detailed and disapproving analysis of *Vimonda* is to be found in: Willard Thorp, 'The Stage Adventures of Some Gothic Novels', *Papers of the Modern Language Association*, XVIII (1928), 479–80.
15. *Prompter*, 27 November 1789.
16. William Capon's notebooks are in the collection of Robert K. Sturtz, New York.
17. James Boaden, *Memoirs of the Life of John Philip Kemble* (1825), II, 101.
18. Thomas Gray, *Mr Gray's Journal* (1775).
19. Joseph Cradock, *An Account of Some of the Most Romantic Parts of North Wales* (1777), p. 1.
20. Radcliffe, *Udolpho*, ed. Dobrée, p. 105.
21. *ibid.*, p. 241.
22. The influence of the gothic novel on the drama is discussed further in: Michael Booth, *English Plays of the Nineteenth Century* (Oxford 1969), I, 24.
23. Ralph G. Allen, 'The Wonders of Derbyshire: A Spectacular Eighteenth Century Travelogue', *Theatre Survey*, II (1961), 54–66.
24. Sybil Rosenfeld and Edward Croft Murray, 'A Checklist of Scene Painters working in Great Britain and Ireland in the Eighteenth-Century', *Theatre Notebook*, XIX (1965), 144–5; Patrick Conner *Michael Angelo Rooker* (1984), pp. 49–93 and 122–37.
25. *European Magazine*, LIV (1808), 391 and XLV (1804), 297.
26. Richard Graves, *The Spiritual Quixote* (1773), ed. Clarence Tracey (1967), p. 186.
27. Humphrey Repton, *Sketches and Hints* (1794), p. 103.
28. Pope's villa at Cross Deep, Twickenham, was demolished in the 1820s by Sophia Howe, 'Queen of the Goths', but the mutilated grotto remains.
29. Horace Walpole, *On Modern Gardening* (1762–71), ed. Wilmarth Sheldon Lewis (New York, 1931), p. 60.
30. William Chambers, *A Dissertation on Oriental Gardening* (Dublin. 1773), p. 27.
31. Chambers, *Oriental Gardening*, p. 28.
32. Whatley's remark is cited in: Lawrence Fleming and Alan Gore, *The English Garden* (1979), p. 109; and Repton's in Peter Bicknell, *Beauty, Horror and Immensity*, Fitzwilliam Museum Exhibition Catalogue (Cambridge, 1981), p. 43.

33. The sentimental garden is discussed in Fleming and Gore's book (see note 32), pp. 85–180.
34. *Theatrical Inquisitor*, II (1813), 64.
35. *Monthly Mirror*, XVI (1809), 117.
36. *The Times*, 25 June 1798; Thomas Dutton, *Dramatic Censor*, I (1800–01), 46.
37. The private theatre in the eighteenth century is described in: Sybil Rosenfeld, *Temples of Thespis* (1978).
38. This subject is fully explored in: F. W. Stokoe, *German Influence in the English Romantic Period* (Cambridge, 1926), pp. 19–34.
39. *British Review*, VIII (1816), 70. Informative biographical details of Charles Maturin are to be found in: Samuel Smiles, *Memoirs and Correspondence of the Late John Murray* (1891), pp. 288–303.
40. *Monthly Review*, LXXX (1816), 179. Further information on the reception of the play is given in: Niilo Idman, *Charles Robert Maturin, His Life and Works* (1923), pp. 102–25.
41. Folger Shakespeare Library, Washington D.C.: letter of Joseph Holman to John Larpent, W. b. 67 (63–63v); Joseph Holman, *The Red Cross Knights* (1799), pp. i–iv; L. W. Conolly, *The Censorship of English Drama* (San Marino, 1976), pp. 98–101.
42. *Monthly Mirror*, IV (1797), 356.
43. Kenneth Woodbridge, 'William Kent's Gardening', *Apollo*, C (1974), pp. 286–9; Margaret Jourdain, *The Work of William Kent* (1984), p. 80. The gothic temple at Shotover is possibly by William Townsend, see: Jennifer Sherwood and Nikolaus Pevsner, *The Buildings of England: Oxfordshire* (1974, rep. 1975), p. 765.
44. Stephen Wright was the architect; wood-carving by a London craftsman, Richard Lawrence; see: Suzanne Mockler, *Milton Manor, Oxfordshire* (n.d.).
45. Bertrand Evans, *Gothic Drama from Walpole to Shelley* (Berkeley and Los Angeles, 1947), p. 5.
46. Hugh Blair, *Lectures on Rhetoric and Belles Lettres* (1787), I, 48–9.
47. Cited in: Samuel H. Monk, *The Sublime. A Study of Critical Theories in Eighteenth Century England* (Michigan, 1960), p. 129.
48. The theme of the beholder's response to the sublime is explored also in: Christopher Hussey, *The Picturesque* (1967) and in Bicknell, *Beauty, Horror and Immensity*.

CHAPTER TWO: A WORLD UNTAMED

1. Julian Charles Young, *A Memoir of Charles Mayne Young* (1871), p. 250. An account of the Grand Tour is to be found in: William Edward Mead, *The Grand Tour in the Eighteenth Century* (Cambridge, 1914).

2. *London Chronicle*, 24–26 April 1766.
3. William Coxe, *Travels in Switzerland* (1789), p. 749.
4. Dolby's British Theatre (1823–25) edn.
5. *The Times*, 15 November 1802.
6. *Monthly Mirror*, XIV (1802), 342.
7. An example of a painter employing this motif is to be seen in: William Payne, 'Landscape with a Waterfall', water-colour and black chalk, Fitzwilliam Museum, Cambridge.
8. William Dimond, *The Broken Sword*, ed. J. Dick (1877).
9. Charles Dibdin the Younger, *The Professional and Literary Memoirs of Charles Dibdin*, ed. George Speaight (1956), p. 99.
10. Cited in: Tate Wilkinson, *Memoirs of His Own Life* (York, 1790), II, 45.
11. Cited in: C. P. Barbier, *William Gilpin* (Oxford, 1963), p. 124.
12. John Genest, *Some Account of the English Stage* (Bath, 1832), VII, 412.
13. *Monthly Mirror*, VIII (1799), 47.
14. Tate Wilkinson, *The Wandering Patentee* (York, 1795), IV, 121.
15. Russell Thomas, 'Contemporary Taste in the Stage Decorations of the London Theatres, 1770–1800', *Modern Philology*, XLII (1944), 71; Jean Georges Noverre, *The Works of Monsieur Noverre translated from the French* (1783), I, 97–8; *Morning Chronicle*, 17 January 1798.
16. Horace Foote, *A Companion to the Theatres* (1829), p. 122.
17. Michael Kelly, *Reminiscences of Michael Kelly* [ed. Theodore Hook] (1926), II, 131.
18. Oswald G. Knapp, *An Artist's Love Story* (1940), p. 184.
19. Thomas West, *A Guide to the Lakes dedicated to Lovers of Landscape Scenery* (1778), *passim*. An early nineteenth-century version of a Claude glass may be seen in the Museum of the History of Science, Oxford.
20. Jane Austen, *Northanger Abbey* (1817), ed. Anne Henry Ehrenpreis (1980), p. 125. An anti-gothic point of view was put by Edward Ferrars in: Jane Austen, *Sense and Sensibility* (1811), ed. James Kingsley and Claire Lamont (Oxford, 1980), p. 84.
21. Cited in Barbier, *Gilpin*, p. 123.
22. A detailed account of the stages at Drury Lane and Covent Garden is given in: *Survey of London* (general editor F. H. W. Sheppard), XXXV (1970), *The Theatre Royal Drury Lane and the Royal Opera House, Covent Garden*; and in Richard Leacroft, *The Development of the English Playhouse* (1973), pp. 107–87.
23. Henry Holland's plans for the Theatre Royal, Drury Lane are in the possession of Robert Edison and reproduced in the *Survey of London*, XXXV, plate 16.
24. An illustrated account of the lighting at the London patent houses

will be found in: Gusta M. Bergman, *Lighting in the Theatre* (Stockholm, 1977) and in: Terence Rees, *Theatre Lighting in the Age of Gas* (1978); see also: Percy Fitzgerald, *The World behind the Scenes* (1881), pp. 13–18 and P. J. Crean, 'Footlights' *Notes and Queries*, CLXIV (1933), 61–2.

25. Cited in: Deryck Lynham, *The Chevalier Noverre* (1972), p. 136.
26. *Annual Register*, VIII (1765), 130.
27. W. J. Lawrence, 'A Forgotten Stage Conventionality', *Anglia*, XXVI (1903), 460.
28. *Public Advertiser*, 14 September 1765.
29. John Joseph Stockdale, *Covent Garden Journal* (1810), p. 59.
30. National Gallery, London.
31. Granville Leveson Gower, *Lord Granville Leveson Gower: Private Correspondence, 1781–1821*, ed. Castalia Granville (1916), I, 245.
32. 'Stage Storms', *All the Year Round*, VIII (1872), 307.
33. Foote, *Companion*, p. 123.
34. *ibid.*
35. 'Stage Storms', *All the Year Round*, VIII, 307.
36. John Gage, 'Loutherbourg: Mystagogue of the Sublime', *History Today*, XIII (1936), 333.
37. de Loutherbourg's experiments in stage design are discussed in: Ralph G. Allen, 'The Stage Spectacles of Philip James de Loutherbourg', unpublished thesis, Yale University, 1960.
38. See, for example, mezzotints by Charles Turner of 'A Shipwreck, 1806' and by Thomas Oldham Barlow of 'The Wreck of the Transport Ship'.
39. *Theatrical Inquisitor* (May, 1816). The prompt-book mentioned is examined by Walter Charles Adelsperger in his unpublished thesis, 'Aspects of the Staging of Plays of the Gothic Revival in England', Ohio State University, 1959.
40. 'Stage Storms', *All the Year Round*, VIII (1872), 304–8.
41. W. H. Pyne, *Wine and Walnuts* (1823), I, 292; Fitzgerald, *Behind the Scenes*, p. 71. See also: Frank Leland Miesle, 'The Staging of Pantomime Entertainments on the London Stage: 1715–1808', unpublished thesis, Ohio State University, 1955, p. 309. Early uses of the storm are discussed by Joseph Addison in the *Spectator*, 20 April 1711. Moulded rollers are portrayed in William Hogarth's engraving, 'Strolling Actresses in a Barn' (1738).
42. Arthur Murphy was theatre critic for the *London Chronicle* for two years from 1757. His approach is discussed in an unpublished thesis by Harvey Marcellus Powers, jnr., 'The Theatrical Criticism of Arthur Murphy, Leigh Hunt and William Hazlitt: A Study in Changing Tastes', Cornell University, 1968.
43. *Spectator*, 24 July 1712; Howard Hunter Dunbar, *The Dramatic*

Career of Arthur Murphy (New York, 1946), p. 215; A. J. C. Hare, *Cities of Southern Italy and Sicily* (Edinburgh, 1883), p. 944.

44. Theatre Museum, London, PB 48 DL. The opening night of this revival was on 3 May 1813.

45. Adelsperger discusses the scenes of this play in his thesis (see n. 39).

46. Kenneth Woodbridge, *The Stourhead Landscape* (1982), pp. 47–50.

47. Elizabeth Wheeler Manwaring, *Italian Landscape in Eighteenth-Century England* (New York, 1925), p. 210. The gardens at Painshill, Cobham, Surrey, were created from 1738 onwards by the Hon. Charles Hamilton. Restoration work on part of the estate is currently undertaken by Elmbridge Council; see: Gwyn Headley and Wim Meulankamp, *Follies* (1986), pp. 109–10 and *The Times*, 17 July 1985.

48. Mary Granville, *The Autobiography and Correspondence of Mary Granville*, ed. Ladly Llanover (1861), II, 492.

49. Coleridge, *Remorse*, 2.2.

50. Novelists, too, owed a debt to Rosa. Ann Radcliffe, for example, based many of her scenic descriptions on his paintings; see: Ernest A. Baker, *History of the English Novel* (1934), V, 197 and Eino Railo, *The Haunted Castle* (1927), p. 26.

51. Cited in: William Gaunt, *Bandits in a Landscape* (1937), p. 40.

52. William Gilpin, *Observations relative chiefly to Picturesque Beauty, Made in the Year 1772 on several Parts of England; particularly the Mountains and Lakes of Cumberland and Westmoreland* (1786), II, 46.

53. Both *The Sicilian Romance* and *Fontainville Forest* are dramatisations of novels by Radcliffe; a consideration of these is made by Roland McClamroch in his unpublished thesis, 'The Gothic Drama', University of Northern Carolina, 1927.

54. Examples of the artificial wilderness (quaint paradox) are shown in John Neale's engraving of Hafod, Cardiganshire and J. C. Stadler's engraving of Clivedon, both in the Ashmolean Museum, Oxford.

55. A discussion of the characteristics of melodrama is to be found in: Michael Booth, *English Melodrama* (1965) and in: William S. Dye, *A Study of Melodrama in England from 1800 to 1840* Pennsylvania (1919).

56. *Lodoiska* as a precursor of melodrama was recognised in the *Monthly Mirror*, XIV (1802), 342; Joseph Donohue in *Theatre in the Age of Kean* (Oxford, 1975), p. 106 accepts *A Tale of Mystery* as the first of the melodramas.

CHAPTER THREE: CASTLE AND CLOISTER

1. Richard Payne Knight, *An Enquiry into the Principles of Taste* (1805), p. 162.
2. The painting is in the National Gallery London. Michael Wilson, *Claude, The Enchanted Castle* (1982), pp. 5, 15, 16.
3. The qualities of Fonthill are discussed in: H. A. N. Brockman, *The Caliph of Fonthill* (1956) and in: David Watkin, *The English Vision* (1982), pp. 102–8.
4. Eastlake, *Gothic Revival*, p. 48.
5. Joseph Burke, *English Art: 1714–1800* (Oxford, 1976), p. 139.
6. John Millington, *Beckford's Tower* (Bath, 1975), p. 9.
7. Richard Brinsley Peake, *Memoirs of the Colman Family* (1841), I, 384.
8. Ann Radcliffe, *The Mysteries of Udolpho* (1794), ed. Bonamy Dobrée (Oxford, 1980), p. 230.
9. A copy of the engraving is in the Theatre Collection of the University of Bristol.
10. Kelly, *Reminiscences*, II, 67.
11. Fitzgerald, *The World behind the Scenes*, p. 3.
12. Foote, *Companion*, p. 123.
13. *The Times*, 10 June 1794.
14. [W. H. Pyne and W. Combe], *The Microcosm of London* (1808–11, rep. 1904), I, 229; Abraham Rees, 'Dramatic Machinery', *The Cyclopaedia or Universal Dictionary of Arts, Sciences and Literature* (1803–19), XII, plate 12.
15. Stone Collection, Theatre Museum; Hodgson and Co., *Hodgson's Sheets of Characters for 'Lodoiska'*. The firm of Hodgson and Co. was situated in the City. Most of the sheets of scenes and characters were issued between 1822 and 1830; see: George Speaight, *The History of the English Toy Theatre* (1946, reissued 1969), pp. 43–4. and 187.
16. Kelly, *Reminiscences*, II, 67; Henry Angelo, *Reminiscences of Henry Angelo* (1825), I, 10–15. A late description of such effects on stage is given in: Olive Logan, 'The Secret Regions of the Stage', *Harpers New Monthly Magazine*, XLVIII (1874), 641.
17. Foote, *Companion*, p. 123.
18. *Monthly Mirror*, XIV (1802), 338.
19. Kelly, *Reminiscences*, II, 67.
20. M. J. Young, *Memoirs of Mrs Crouch* (1806), II, 215.
21. *Monthly Mirror*, VII (1799), 47 and 113.
22. Boaden, *Kemble*, II, 231.

23. *Gentleman's Magazine*, LXIX (1799), 114–15. 'Antiquary' may be the *nom-de-plume* of John Carter.
24. Walpole, *Letters*, ed. Toynbee, VI, 388.
25. Herbert Butterfield, *History and Human Relations* (1951), p. 244.
26. The gothic castle is discussed in: Railo, *The Haunted Castle*, pp. 79–136.
27. The notion of the sublimity of the villain is put forward in: Marlies K. Danziger, 'Heroic Villains in Eighteenth-Century Criticism', *Comparative Literature*, II (1959), 40–4.
28. The freedom metaphor and iconography is discussed in: Lorenz Eitner, 'Cages, Prisons and Captives in Eighteenth-Century Art', *Images of Romanticism*, ed. Karl Kroeber and William Walling (New Haven, 1978), pp. 13–35.
29. David Jarrett, *The Gothic Form in Fiction and its Relation to History* (Winchester, 1980), p. 4.
30. John Montagu, *A Voyage Performed by the Late Earl of Sandwich Round the Mediterranean in the Years 1738 and 1739* (1799), pp. 22–3.
31. Giovanni Piranesi, *Carceri d'Invenzione* (Rome, 1761).
32. Horace Walpole, *Anecdotes of Painting in England* (1762–71), ed. R. N. Wornum (1876), I, xvi.
33. *Gentleman's Magazine*, LXXI (1801), 409.
34. *European Magazine*, XXXIX (1801), 359.
35. [Margaret Baron-Wilson], *The Life and Correspondence of M. G. Lewis* (1839), II, 56–7; Walley Chamberlain Oulton, *A History of the Theatres of London* (1818), II, 58.
36. *The Times*, 2 December 1808.
37. [Baron-Wilson], *Lewis*, II, 58; Peter Winn, 'Multiple Settings on the Early Nineteenth-Century Stage', *Theatre Notebook*, XXXV (1981), 23.
38. *The Times*, 13 December 1808.
39. Matthew Gregory Lewis, *Venoni* (1809), pp. 59–86.
40. Laurence Sterne, *A Sentimental Journey* (1748), ed. W. R. Cross (New York, 1926), p. 108.
41. Ann Radcliffe, *The Castles of Athlin and Dunbayne* (1789) and *A Sicilian Romance* (1790).
42. George Colman the Younger, *Blue-Beard* (1798), iii–vi.
43. Michael Kelly, *The Grand Dramatic Romance of 'Blue-Beard or Female Curiosity' as now performing at the Theatre Royal, Drury Lane with Unbounded Applause, the Words by George Colman the Younger, Esq., the music composed and selected by Michael Kelly* (1798), front cover; *Monthly Mirror*, V (1798), 45.

44. Leacroft, *English Playhouse*, p. 141; *London Chronicle*, 18 January 1798.
45. Playbill for a performance of *Blue-Beard* at the Theatre Royal, Brighton, 23 June 1815, reproduced in: Mary Teresa Odell, *Mr Trotter of Worthing and the Brighton Theatre* (Aylesbury, 1944), p. 36.
46. *London Chronicle*, 18 January 1798.
47. Kelly, *Reminiscences*, II, 146–7.
48. Charles Dickens, *Memoirs of Joseph Grimabldi* (1838), ed. Richard Findlater (1968), p. 88.
49. *The Benedictine Year Book*, ed. Gordon Beattie (York, 1982), pp. 62 and 172.
50. Richard Colt Hoare, *Recollections Abroad* (Bath, 1815–18), IV, 75.
51. Samuel Rogers, *The Italian Journal of Samuel Rogers*, ed. J. R. Hale (1956), p. 240; Samuel Rogers, *Italy, a Poem* (1839), p. 196.
52. *Gentleman's Magazine*, XCVII (1827), 374–5.
53. Thomas Campbell, *Life of Mrs Siddons* (1834), II, 255.
54. *Star*, 1 May 1800; *London Packet*, 28–30 April 1800.
55. *Quarterly Review*, XXXIV (1826), 230; Thomas Holcroft, *Memoirs of the Late Thomas Holcroft*, ed. William Hazlitt (1816), I, 273.
56. See, for example, the review in *The Times*, 30 April 1800.
57. Dutton, *Dramatic Censor*, II, 133.
58. Michael Kelly, cited in the *Gentleman's Magazine*, XCVIII (1828), 106.
59. Young, *Crouch*, II, 303; Boaden, *Jordan*, II, 7. Responses to *The Monk* are considered in: Edith Birkhead, *The Tale of Terror* (1963), pp. 66–9.
60. *Gentleman's Magazine*, LXXI (1801), 410.
61. *ibid.*, p. 409; *European Magazine*, XXXIX (1801), 359.
62. *Gentleman's Magazine*, LXXII (1802), 328. Further details of this setting and of Capon's work generally are given in: *Gentleman's Magazine*, XCVII (1827), 234–377 and XCVIII (1828), 105–7; Sybil Rosenfeld, *Georgian Scene Painters and Scene Painting* (Cambridge, 1981), p. 100; Ralph G. Allen, 'Capon's Scenes for Melodrama', *Theatre Research*, VIII (1966), 7–17.
63. Print Room, British Museum: Turner, 'Llanthony Abbey', pencil and watercolour, Turner Bequest 27.
64. William Mason, *The English Garden* (1771), p. 1.
65. Arthur Young, *Six Month's Tour of the North* (1770–71), cited in: [Gervase Jackson-Stops], *The Rievaulx Terrace* (1982), p. 14.
66. Cited in: Roger Fiske, *English Theatre Music in the Eighteenth Century* (1973), p. 554.
67. John Hadfield, ed., *The Shell Guide to England* (1970, rep. 1973), p. 275.

CHAPTER FOUR: THE STAGE SPECTACLE

1. Frederick Reynolds, *The Life and Times of Frederick Reynolds* (1826), II, 55.
2. Pyne, *Wine and Walnuts*, I, 286.
3. *Gentleman's Magazine*, LXIX (1799), 114.
4. James Robinson Planché, *A History of British Costume* (1834), p. xi.
5. Boaden, *Kemble*, I, 75.
6. Charles Beecher Hogan, 'The Theatre of George III', *Horace Walpole, Writer, Politician and Connoisseur*, ed. Warren Hunting Smith (1967), p. 229.
7. Fitzgerald, *Kembles*, I, 323.
8. Sarah Siddons, *The Reminiscences of Sarah Kemble Siddons*, ed. William Van Lennep (Cambridge, Mass., 1942), pp. 19–20.
9. Theatre Museum, London: 'Mrs Siddons as Euphrasia', engraving after a painting by William Hamilton.
10. Print Room, British Museum, London: Mary Hamilton, Watercolours, 201. b. 10., ff. 24 and 25.
11. *Theatrical Inquisitor*, III (1814), 343.
12. *ibid*, II (1813), 100; Holcroft, *Memoirs*, I, 273.
13. British Library: 'Collection of cuttings referring to Drury Lane', 11795. k. 22.
14. Archive Collection of the Royal Opera House, Covent Garden: playbill, *The Exile*, 24 September 1810.
15. Frederick Reynolds, *The Exile*, ed. D. G. [George Daniel] (n.d.).
16. Rosenfeld, *Georgian Scene Painters*, p. 93.
17. Archive Collection of the Royal Opera House: anonymous engraving, 'Scene in the New Tragedy of *The Law of Lombardy*, Mr Henderson, Mr Smith and Miss Young in the Characters of Bireno, Paladore and the Prisoner'.
18. See, for example, *The Times*, 23 July 1798, for the supernatural in *The Cambro-Britons*; European Magazine, XXXIX (1801), 359, for the ghost in *Adelmorn the Outlaw* and *Theatre*, 10 July 1819, for the ghost in *The Bride of Lammermuir*.
19. Walpole, *Letters*, ed. Toynbee, X, 206.
20. Print Room, British Museum: West, *et al.*, 'Scenes and Figures for Toy Theatres' (1811), f. 281
21. Matthew Gregory Lewis, *Raymond and Agnes*, ed. J. Dicks (n.d.).
22. Boaden, *Kemble*, II, 117 and 119.
23. Fitzgerald, *The World behind the Scenes*, p. 18.
24. Oulton, *London Theatres*, II, 17.
25. Rosenfeld and Croft Murray, 'Checklist', *Theatre Notebook*, XIX, (1964), 14 and *The Times*, 23 January 1813.

26. See, for example: *The Times*, 25 January 1813. Not everyone agreed with this criticism. William Hazlitt, considering the literary rather than the theatrical potential, spoke of the 'wild harp of poetry' softening the 'sterner voice of the tragic muse', see: Hazlitt, *Works*, ed. Howe, XVIII, 463.
27. *Examiner*, 24 March 1811.
28. Gower, *Corrrespondence*, I, 120
29. *Examiner*, 24 March 1811.
30. John Williams, *Dramatic Censor* (1811), p. 153.
31. Boaden, *Kemble*, II, 543.
32. Louis Simond, *An American in Regency England*, ed. Christopher Hibbert (1968), p. 130.
33. *Examiner*, 24 March 1811.
34. William Webb, *Webb's Characters in 'Blue-Beard'* (n.d.), pl. 3; J. Bailey and Co., *Plates for Blue-Beard* (n.d.).
35. Genest, *English Stage*, VIII, 232.
36. *The Times*, 30 April 1811.
37. Robinson, *London Theatre*, p. 35.
38. William Pitt Lennox, *My Recollections from 1806 to 1873* (1874), I, 168.
39. *European Magazine*, LIX (1811), 378
40. *Jackson's Oxford Journal*, 23 September 1815.
41. *European Magazine*, LXIV (1813), 335.
42. Archive Collection of the Royal Opera House: playbill, *The Miller and His Men*, 28 October 1813.
43. Theatre Museum, Stone Collection: various toy theatre sheets.
44. Noverre's role in the unification of stage spectacle is discussed by Ralph Thomas in 'Contemporary Taste in the Stage Decorations of London Theatres, 1770–1800', *Modern Philology*, XLII (1944), 66–7.
45. de Loutherbourg's letters of proposal are in the Forster Collection in the Library of the Victoria and Albert Museum. A translation, used here, by Russell Thomas is to be found in: 'Loutherbourg's Letters to Garrick', *Drama Critique*, IX (1966), 42–4.
46. *Gazetteer*, 13 December 1779; *Westminster Magazine*, VII (1779), 654.
47. An example, typical of de Loutherbourg's work is 'Smugglers landing in a Storm' in the Victoria Art Gallery, Bath. His work is illustrated in: Rudiger Joppien, *Philippe Jacques de Loutherbourg, R.A., 1740–1812*, Greater London Council/Kenwood House exhibition catalogue (1973).
48. Richard Cumberland, *Supplement to the Memoirs of Richard Cumberland* (1807), p. 57.

49. Holland mss., cited by: Richard Leacroft, *The Development of the English Playhouse* (1973), p. 148.
50. Andrew Saint, *et al.*, *A History of the Royal Opera House, Covent Garden, 1732–1982* (1982), p. 15.
51. Cumberland, *Supplement to the Memoirs*, p. 58; *Survey of London*, XXXV, 57–65, 93–6.
52. George Gordon Byron, *Byron's Letters and Journals*, ed. Leslie Marchand, IV (1975), 296–7; Rees, *Theatre Lighting*, pp. 9–10.
53. Joanna Baillie, *A Series of Plays in which it is attempted to delineate the stronger passions of the mind* (1821), III, xxvi.
54. Theatre Museum: prompt book for a revival in 1817 of *A Tale of Mystery*, PB 203 DL.

CHAPTER FIVE: ATTITUDE AND SPEECH

1. Benjamin Robert Haydon, *The Autobiography and Memoirs of Benjamin Robert Haydon, 1786–1846*, ed. Tom Taylor (1926), I, 362.
2. Joshua Reynolds, *Discourses on Art* (1778), ed. Robert R. Wark (1975), p. 101.
3. Nicholas Penny, ed. *Reynolds*, Royal Academy of Art Exhibition Catalogue (1986), pp. 26–9 and 32. Dulwich Picture Gallery: Joshua Reynolds, 'Mrs Siddons as the Tragic Muse', 1789.
4. Henry Siddons, *Practical Illustrations of Rhetorical Gesture and Action* (1807).
5. Siddons, *Rhetorical Gesture* (second edition, 1822), p. 14.
6. Emma Hamilton, mistress, then wife, of Sir William Hamilton, British ambassador in Naples, gave demonstrations of dramatic attitudes which are illustrated in Frederick Rehberg, *Drawings Faithfully Copied from Nature at Naples* (1794). These, together with the employment of attitudes by actors are discussed in: K. G. Holmström, *Monodrama, Attitudes, Tableaux Vivants* (Stockholm, 1967).
7. Frederick Reynolds, *The Life and Times of Frederick Reynolds* (1826), I, 151.
8. William Stone, *The Beauties of the Stage* (1792), p. vii.
9. Thomas Davies, *Memoirs of the Life of David Garrick* (1808), II, 358.
10. Peake, *Colman Family*, II, 20; Thomas Morris, *Miscellanies in Prose and Verse* (1791), p. 52.
11. Boaden, *Siddons*, II, 49.
12. *Cork Chronicle*, 16 September 1765.
13. Cited in: John Alexander Kelly, *German Visitors to English Theatres in the Eighteenth-Century* (Princeton, 1936), p. 141.
14. Bertram Joseph, *The Tragic Actor* (1959), p. 247.
15. Boaden, *Jordan*, II, 23.

16. *ibid.*, II, 16–17.
17. *ibid.*
18. Leigh Hunt, *Autobiography of Leigh Hunt* (1850), ed. Roger Ingpen (New York), 1903, p. 152.
19. William Hazlitt, *Dramatic Essays*, ed. William Archer and Robert Lowe (1895), p. 119.
20. A remark recorded by John Foster and quoted in: William Shakespeare, *Richard III*, ed. Alan Downer (1959), p. xvii.
21. Jesse Foot, *The Life of Arthur Murphy, Esq.* (1811), p. 222.
22. John Galt, *The Lives of the Players* (1831), II, 125.
23. Simond, *An American in Regency England*, ed. Hibbert, p. 46.
24. Boaden, *Siddons*, I, 312.
25. Wilkinson, *Wandering Patentee*, II, 197.
26. Cited in: *The English Dramatic Critics*, ed. James Agate, [1932], p. 70.
27. Campbell, *Siddons*, I, 169.
28. Cited in: *English Dramatic Critics*, p. 70.
29. Boaden, *Siddons*, I, 312.
30. Sarah and William Siddons, *The Letters of Sarah and William Siddons to Hester Lynch Piozzi in the John Ryland Library*, ed. Kalman A. Burnim (Manchester, 1969), p. 49.
31. Kelly, *German Visitors*, p. 145.
32. Wilkinson, *Wandering Patentee*, III, 98.
33. Cooke, *Macklin*, p. 174.
34. [Haslewood], *Green Room*, I, 51.
35. *Morning Chronicle*, 30 November 1772.
36. Dutton, *Dramatic Censor*, II, 257.
37. Sarah Siddons's performances are discussed in the unpublished thesis of Patricia M. McMohan, 'The Tragical Art of Sarah Siddons', University of Yale, 1972.
38. Baillie, *A Series of Plays*, I, xxxiv–lxvi.
39. Campbell, *Siddons*, II, 254.
40. Baillie, *De Monfort*, ed. Inchbald, p. 4; Anna Seward, *Letters of Anna Seward*, ed. A. Constable (Edinburgh, 1811), V, 243.
41. Joanna Baillie, *Dramatic Works* (1851), p. x
42. Joanna Baillie, *The Works of Joanna Baillie* (1853), p. xi.
43. Hazlitt, *Works*, ed. Howe, V, 147.
44. Dutton, *Dramatic Censor*, II, 132.
45. Siddons, *Rhetorical Gesture*, p. 14.
46. Baillie, *A Series of Plays*, p. xxx.
47. *ibid.*, p. xxix.
48. *ibid.*, p. xxi.
49. Cited in: Margaret S. Cahart, *The Life and Work of Joanna Baillie* (New Haven, 1923), p. 101.

50. Hazlitt, *Works*, ed. Howe, V, 304.
51. Cited in: H. Barton Baker, *The London Stage* (1889), I, 215–16.
52. John Taylor, 'The Stage' in John Ambrose Williams, *Memoir of John Philip Kemble, Esq.* (1817), p. 60.
53. Gower, *Correspondence*, ed. Granville, I, 481; Hunt, *Dramatic Essays*, ed. Archer and Lowe, p. 7.
54. Taylor, 'The Stage' in Williams, *Kemble*, p. 60.
55. Anthony Pasquin, *The Children of Thespis* (1792), p. 48.
56. *The Times*, 28 Novembeer 1821; F. W. Hawkins, *The Life of Edmund Kean* (1869), II, 181.
57. Widener Library, Harvard University: Shaw Theatre Collection, letter of Joanna Baillie.
58. Genest, *English Stage*, IX, 177.
59. Hawkins, *Kean*, II, 181.

CHAPTER SIX: THREE CASE STUDIES

1. The first performance of *Douglas* was on 14 December 1756 at the Cannongate Theatre in Edinburgh. An example of the enthusiastic response to the play is seen in the article by 'Crito' in the *Edinburgh Evening Courant*, 18 December 1756.
2. John Home, *Douglas* (Belfast, 1757).
3. *Critical Review*, III (1757), 267.
4. *London Chronicle*, 12–15 March 1757.
5. Henry Mackenzie, *An Account of the Life and Writings of John Home* (Edinburgh, 1822), pp. 100–1.
6. *London Chronicle*, 14 March 1757.
7. John Jackson, *The History of the Scottish Stage* (Edinburgh, 1793), pp. 331–2.
8. Wilkinson, *Wandering Patentee*, II, 240.
9. John Bernard, *Retrospections of the Stage* (Boston, 1832), I, 174. The Barrett mentioned is possibly Giles Linnett Barrett.
10. *Morning Chronicle*, 14 November 1783.
11. Jackson, *Scottish Stage*, p. 331.
12. Cited in: Genest, *English Stage*, IV, 489.
13. Portraits of Betty in the role of Young Norval were painted by James Northcott and John Opie.
14. William and Dorothy Wordsworth, *Letters of William and Dorothy Wordsworth*, ed. Edward de Selincourt (Oxford, 1967), I, 519.
15. Hazlitt, *Works*, ed. Howe, VIII, 294.
16. Boaden, *Kemble*, II, 400 and 403; *The Life of William Henry West Betty* (1804), p. 6.
17. James Solas Dodd, *Critical Remarks on Mrs Jackson's performance*

of Lady Randolph in the Tragedy of 'Douglas' at the Theatre Royal in Covent Garden (1779), p. 41.

18. William Macready, *The Reminiscences of William Macready*, ed. Frederick Pollock (1875), I, 56.

19. John Doran, *Their Majesties' Servants. Annals of the English Stage* (1864), II, 343; Campbell, *Siddons*, I, 50; Boaden, *Siddons*, II, 51.

20. Dodd, *Critical Remarks*, p. 44.

21. *Public Advertiser*, 7 May 1784; *Morning Post*, 9 January 1788.

22. Macready, *Reminiscences*, I, 56.

23. Cited in Genest, *English Stage*, IV, 489.

24. Dodd, *Critical Remarks*, p. 45.

25. Macready, *Reminiscences*, I, 57.

26. Hester Piozzi, *Intimate Letters of Hester Piozzi and Penelope Pennington, 1788–1821*, ed. Oswald G. Knapp (1913), p. 91.

27. William Dunlap, *Memoirs of George Frederick Cooke* (1813), I, 29.

28. David Hume, *Four Dissertations* (1757), pp. v–vi.

29. *Caledonian Mercury*, 19 April 1787.

30. D. E. Baker, *Biographia Dramatica*, ed. Stephen Jones (1812), I, 360n. Audience responses to *Douglas* are discussed in : Alice Edna Gipson, *John Home, a Study of his Life and Works* (New Haven, 1916), pp. 36–95; St Vincent Troubridge and L. R. M. Strachan, 'The Success of *Douglas*', *Notes and Queries*, CLXXXI (1941), 148–9; 163.

31. 'Solomon Grildrig of Eton College', *The Miniature* (1860), pp. 281–5. Is the performance satirised one given by the Margravine of Anspach and her son, the Hon Keppel Craven, at either the private theatre of Brandenburg House, Hammersmith, or in her garden theatre at Benham Park, Newbury? There are some resemblances to contemporary descriptions.

32. William Makepeace Thackeray, *The Virginians* (1858; third edition, 1863), p. 616.

33. *Monthly Mirror*, VII (1797), 355–6.

34. Matthew Gregory Lewis, *The Castle Spectre* (1797), p. 102.

35. The oil-painting is in the collection at Firle Place, Sussex.

36. Campbell, *Siddons*, II, 282.

37. *Monthly Visitor*, II (1797), 537.

38. Young, *Crouch*, II, 285.

39. Lewis, *The Castle Spectre*, p. 71n.

40. *European Magazine*, XXXIII (1798), 42.

41. *True Briton*, 16 December 1797.

42. Department of Manuscripts, British Library: Memoranda of John Philip Kemble, BL Addl ms 31973 II, entry for 14 December 1797.

43. Rosenfeld and Croft Murray, 'Checklist', *Theatre Notebook*, XIX (1964), 59.

44. *Gentleman's Magazine*, LXIX (1799), 469.
45. Boaden, *Kemble*, II, 207.
46. Summers, *The Gothic Quest*, p. 203.
47. *Gentleman's Magazine*, LXIX (1797), 470.
48. The use of this motif is explored in: David Jarrett 'A Source for Keats' Magic Casements', *Notes and Queries*, CCIV (1979), 232–5.
49. Boaden, *Jordan*, I, 347–8.
50. Cited by Adelsperger, 'Aspects of Staging Plays of the Gothic Revival', p. 75.
51. Ellis, *Kelly*, pp. 25–2.
52. Boaden, *Jordan*, I, 347–8.
53. *European Magazine*, XXXIII (1798), 42.
54. An instance occurred at the Theatre Royal, Plymouth; a playbill for 16 June 1802 advertised a 'Transparency of a Roman Oratory with a Grand and Awful Appearance of the Spectre of the Castle'; see: Harvey Crane, *Playbill* (Plymouth, 1980), p. 66.
55. See, for example: *Monthly Mirror*, V (1798), 113.
56. Matthew Gregory Lewis, *The Monk* (1794).
57. Siddons, *Rhetorical Gesture*, p. 88.
58. *Monthly Mirror*, VII (1799), 192.
59. Folger Shakespeare Library, Washington.
60. Laurence Sterne, *The Sentimental Journey* (1768), ed. Graham Petrie (1967), p. 98.
61. [Baron-Wilson], *Lewis*, I, 72.
62. *Monthly Visitor*, II, (1797), 537; Thomas Sedgwick Whalley, *Journals and Correspondence of Thomas Sedgwick Whalley, D.D.*, ed. Hill Wickham (1863), II, 108.
63. Young, *Crouch*, II, 282.
64. *Morning Herald*, 16 December 1797; *Monthly Mirror*, IV (1797), 356 and (1798), 113.
65. George Gordon Byron, 'English Bards and Scottish Reviewers', in *The Poetical Works of Lord Byron* (1959), p. 125.
66. Samuel Taylor Coleridge, *The Letters of Samuel Taylor Coleridge*, ed. Earl Leslie Griggs (Oxford, 1959), letter 225.
67. *Gentleman's Magazine*, LXIX (1799), 469 and 471.
68. *The Times*, 19 December 1797.
69. James Gillray drew a cartoon of Sheridan as Pizarro, raking in the wealth which the stage presentation made for him.
70. A study of Rolla as the 'Artificial Hero' is to be found in Donohue, *Dramatic Character*, pp. 125–56.
71. Thomas More, *Memoirs of the Life of the Rt. Hon. Richard Brinsley Sheridan* (1825), p. 582.
72. John Johnson Collection, Bodleian Library, Oxford: playbill, *Pizarro*, 5 April 1800.

73. This occurrred, for example, at the Chelmsford Theatre; the manager's puff claimed that Ataliba's costume alone cost 40 gns. See: *Chelmsford Chronicle*, 26 July and 2 August 1799.

74. Folger Shakespeare Library, Washington: prompt book, based on third edition of *Pizarro*, signed 'J. Kemble' on the fly-leaf. Charles Shattock in *The Kemble Promptbooks* (Washington, 1974), II, 5, suggests that the prompt book may be a written record of a later production at Covent Garden.

75. Print Room, British Museum: Designs of John Henderson Grieve, verso 23, 200 + c 7.

76. M. and B. Skelt, *Skelt's Scenes in 'Pizarro'* [1850], no. 1.

77. *The Times*, 25 May 1799.

78. Folger Shakespeare Library, Washington: 'A Peruvian's Vengeance', anonymous engraving; Bristol University Collection: 'Mr Young as Rolla in *Pizarro*', engraving published by B. Perkins.

79. Moore, *Sheridan*, p. 583; John Watkins, *Memoirs of the Public and Private Life of the Rt. Hon. R. B. Sheridan with a Particular Account of his Family and Connexions* (1817), II, 292. A discussion on the origins of some of the speeches in *Pizarro* is given in: John Loftis, *Sheridan and the Drama of Georgian England* (1976), pp. 124–141.

80. Piozzi, *Intimate Letters*, p. 178.

81. *Enchiridion Clericum* (1812), p. 70.

82. *The Stage* (1815–16), p. 267.

83. Michael Kelly, *The Music of 'Pizzaro'* (1799).

84. [Thomas Dutton], *Pizarro in Peru or The Death of Rolla* [1799], p. 53; Skelt, *The Scenes in 'Pizarro'*, no. 5.

85. Folger Shakespeare Library, Washington: prompt book, *Pizarro*.

86. *ibid.*

87. [Dutton], *Pizarro in Peru*, p. 75.

88. Print Room, British Museum: watercolour drawing by Mary Hamilton.

89. [Dutton], *Pizarro in Peru*, p. 105.

90. Archive Collection of the Royal Opera House, Covent Garden: George III at a performance of Pizarro, engraving.

91. Lawrence's painting is owned by the Kansas City Art Institute and displayed in the William Rockhill Nelson Gallery of Art.

92. Boaden, *Kemble*, II, 240.

93. Oulton, *Theatres of London*, I, 54.

94. Folger Shakespeare Library, Washington: prompt book, *Pizarro*.

95. Kelly, *The Music of Pizarro*, p. 30.

96. Oulton, *Theatres of London*, I, 54; *Morning Chronicle*, 25 and 27 May 1799; *True Briton*, 27 May 1799; *The Times*, 29 May 1799.

97. As an example see: *European Magazine*, XXXV (1799), 402.

98. Percy Fitzgerald, *A New History of the English Stage* (1882), II, 21.
99. William Gifford, *The Baviad and the Maeviad* (1811), p. 62n.
100. *Anti-Jacobin Review*, III (1799), 208.
101. [Dutton], *Pizarro in Peru*, p. 117.

CHAPTER SEVEN: THE RESPONSE TO THE GOTHIC DRAMA

1. *Quarterly Review*, XXXIV (1826), 198.
2. *ibid.*, p. 199.
3. Doran, *Their Majesties' Servants*, II, 414; Frederick Howard; *Thoughts upon the Present Condition of the Stage* (1809), p. 87; Boaden, *Kemble*, II, 403.
4. Boaden, *Kemble*, II, 403.
5. *European Magazine*, XLVII (1805), 373.
6. British Library: 'Biographies of Actors, etc.', BL. Th. Cts. 75.
7. Hannah Cowley, *The Town before You* (1795), p. x.
8. *Theatrical Inquisitor*, X (1817), 381–2.
9. This actress may be Ann Johnstone.
10. Knight, *Principles of Taste*, pp. 354 5.
11. *The Times*, 25 June 1792. It is not clear to which Miss de Camp the writer is referring. This may be Maria Theresa de Camp.
12. Oulton, *Theatres of London*, I, 7.
13. Carl Philipp Moritz, *The Travels of Carl Philipp Moritz in England in 1782* (1795), ed. P.E. Matheson (1924), p. 76.
14. Oliver Goldsmith, 'An Essay on the Theatre' in *The Collected Works of Oliver Goldsmith*, ed. Arthur Friedman (Oxford, 1966), III, 213.
15. William Dunlap, *A History of the American Theatre* (New York, 1832), p. 105.
16. Knight, *Principles of Taste*, p. 340.
17. *European Magazine*, III (1783), 147; *Town and Country Magazine*, XV (1783), 95.
18. Hester Lynch Thrale, *Thraliana. The Diary of Mrs Hester Lynch Thrale*, ed. Katharine C. Balderston (Oxford, 1961), p. 713.
19. *Monthly Record*, LXXX (1816), 187.
20. W. Torrens McCullagh, *Memoirs of the Rt. Hon. Richard Lalor Sheil* (1855), pp. 117–18.
21. Hazlitt, *Works*, ed. Howe, XII, 365.
22. Dutton, *Dramatic Censore*, IV, 193.
23. *ibid.*, IV, 194.
24. Manuscript Department, British Library: Memoranda of John Philip Kemble, BL Add. Ms. 31924, III, entry for 25 April 1810.
25. This judgement is discussed in MacDonald Emslie, 'Home's *Douglas*

and Wully Shakespeare', *Studies in Scottish Literature*, II (1964); Arnold Lätt, *Robert Jephson and his Tragedies* (Zurich 1913), p. 60.

26. See, for example: Edmund John Eyre, *The Fatal Sisters* (1797), Prefatory Address; William Dunlap, *The Diary of William Dunlap. 1766–1839*, ed. Dorothy C. Barck (New York 1930), entry for 30 October 1819.

27. Irish Murdoch, *The Bell* (1958).

Bibliography and Other Sources

1. PRINTED BOOKS AND ARTICLES

Aikin, John and Barbauld, Anna Letitia, *Miscellaneous Pieces in Prose*, 1792.

Allen, B. Sprague, *Tides in English Taste*, Cambridge, Mass., 1937.

Allen, Ralph G., 'Capon's scenes for melodrama', *Theatre Research*, VIII (1966), 7–17.

'Kemble and Capon at Drury Lane, 1794 1802', *Educational Theatre Journal*, XXIII (1971), 22–35.

Ashton, Geoffrey and Mackintosh, Iain, *Royal Opera House Retrospective, 1732–1982*, 1982, exhibition catalogue.

Aubin, Robert A., 'Grottoes, Geology and the Gothic Revival', *Studies in Philology*, XXXI (1934), 408–16.

Austen, Jane, *Northanger Abbey*, 1818, ed. Anne Henry Ehrenpreis, 1980.

Baker, D. E., *Biographia Dramatica*, ed. Stephen Jones, 1812.

Baker, Ernest A., *A History of the English Novel*, 1924–1939.

Baker, H. Barton, *The London Stage*, 1889.

Baker, Herschel, *John Philip Kemble: the Actor in his Theatre*, Cambridge, Mass., 1942.

Barbier, Carl Paul, *William Gilpin*, Oxford, 1963.

[Baron-Wilson, Margaret], *The Life and Correspondence of M. G. Lewis*, 1839.

Bergman, Gusta M., *Lighting in the Theatre*, Stockholm, 1977.

Bicknell, Peter, *Beauty, Horror and Immensity*, Cambridge, 1981, exhibition catalogue.

Birkhead, Edith, *The Tale of Terror*, New York, 1963.

Bisset, John, ed., *Critical Essays on the Dramatic Excellencies of the Young Roscius*, 1804.

Blair, Hugh, *Lectures on Rhetoric and Belles Lettres*, 1787.

Boaden, James, *The Life of Mrs Jordan*, 1831.

Memoirs of the Life of John Philip Kemble, 1815.

Memoirs of Mrs Siddons, 1827.

Booth, Michael, ed., *English Plays of the Nineteenth Century*, Oxford, 1969–73.

Burke, Edmund, *A Philosophical Enquiry into the Origin of our Ideas of the Sublime and Beautiful*, 1759.

Campbell, Thomas, *The Life of Mrs Siddons*, 1834.

Carhart, Margaret S., *The Life and Work of Joanna Baillie*, New Haven, Conn., 1923.

Chambers, William, *A Dissertation on Oriental Gardening*, Dublin, 1773.

Conner, Patrick, *Michael Angelo Rooker*, 1984.

Danzigger, Marlies K., 'Heroic Villains in Eighteenth-Century Criticism', *Comparative Literature*, XI (1959), 35–46.

Dibdin the Elder, Charles, *A Complete History of the Stage*, 1797–1800.

Dodd, J.S., *Critical Remarks on Mrs Jackson's Performance of Lady Randolph in the Tragedy of 'Douglas' at the Theatre Royal in Covent Garden*, 1779.

Donohue, Joseph W., *Dramatic Character in the English Romantic Age*, Princeton, 1970.

Theatre in the Age of Kean, Oxford, 1975.

'Hazlitt's Sense of the Dramatic: Actor as Tragic Character', *Studies in English Literature*, V (1965), 705–21.

Doran, John, *Their Majesties' Servants. Annals of the English Stage*, 1864.

'Charles Farley', *Notes and Queries*, VII (1859), 143–4.

Downer, Alan S., 'Nature to Advantage Dressed', *Publications of the Modern Language Association of America*, LVIII (1943), 1002–37.

'Players and Painted Stage', *Publications of the Modern Language Association of America*, LXI (1946), 522–76.

Dunbar, Howard Hunter, *The Dramatic Career of Arthur Murphy*, New York, 1946.

[Dutton, Thomas], *Pizarro in Peru*, 1799.

Dye, William S., *A Study of Melodrama in England from 1800 to 1840*, Pennsylvania, 1919.

Ellis, Stewart Marsh, *The Life of Michael Kelly*, 1930.

Emslie, Macdonald, 'Home's *Douglas* and Wully Shakespeare', *Studies in Scottish Literature*, II (1964), 128–9.

Evans, Bertrand, *Gothic Drama from Walpole to Shelley*, Berkeley and Los Angeles, 1947.

ffrench, Yvonne, *Mrs Siddons: Tragic Actress*, 1936.

Fiske, Roger, *English Theatre Music in the Eighteenth Century*, 1973.

Fitzgerald, Percy, *The Kembles*, 1871.

The World behind the Scenes, 1881.

Fleming, Laurence and Gore, Alan, *The English Garden*, 1979.

Foot, Jesse, *The Life of Arthur Murphy*, 1811.

Foote, Horace, *A Companion to the Theatres*, 1829.

Gage, John, 'Loutherbourg: Mystagogue of the Sublime', *History Today*, XIII (1963), 332–9.

Gaunt, William, *Bandits in a Landscape*, 1937.

Genest, John, *Some Account of the English Stage*, Bath, 1832.

Gilpin, William, *Three Essays: On Picturesque Beauty, on Picturesque Travel and on Sketching Landscape*, 1794.

Gipson, Alice Edna, *John Home. A Study of his Life and Works*, New Haven, Conn., 1916.

Hazlitt, William, *The Complete Works of William Hazlitt*, ed. P. P. Howe, 1930–34.

Hedley, Gill, *The Picturesque Tour in Northumberland and Durham*, c 1720–1830, Newcastle upon Tyne, 1982, exhibition catalogue.

Hibbert, Christopher, *The Grand Tour*, 1987.

Highfill, Phillip H. jnr., *et al, A Biographical Dictionary of Actors, Actresses, Musicians, Dancers, Managers and Other Stage Personnel in London, 1660–1800*, Carbondale, from 1973.

Holmström, K. G., *Monodrama, Attitudes, Tableaux Vivants*, Stockholm, 1967.

Hume, David, *Four Dissertations: The Natural History of Religion; Of the Passions; Of Tragedy; Of the Standard of Taste*, 1757.

Hussey, Christopher, *The Picturesque*, 1967.

Jackson, John, *The History of the Scottish Stage*, Edinburgh, 1793.

Jarrett, David, *The Gothic Form in Fiction and its Relation to History*, Winchester, 1980.

Jones, Barbara, *Follies and Grottoes*, 1974.

Joppien, Rüdiger, *Philippe Jacques de Loutherbourg, R.A., 1740–1812*, 1973, exhibition catalogue.

Joseph, Bertram, *The Tragic Actor*, 1959.

Kelly, John Alexander, *German Visitors to English Theatres in the Eighteenth Century*, Princeton, 1936.

Kelly, Linda, *The Kemble Era*, 1980.

Kelly, Michael, *Reminiscences of Michael Kelly*, ed. Theodore Hook, 1826.

Kitson, Michael, *Salvator Rosa*, 1973, exhibition catalogue.

Knight, Richard Payne, *An Enquiry into the Principles of Taste*, 1805.

Latt, Arnold, *Robert Jephson and his Tragedies*, Zurich, 1913.

Lawrence, William J., 'A Forgotten Stage Conventionality', *Anglia*, XXVI (1903), 459–61.

'The Pioneers of Modern English Stage Mounting: William Capon', *Magazine of Art*, No 176 (1895), 289–92.

'Stage Scenery in the Eighteenth Century', *Magazine of Art*, No. 178 (1895), 385–8.

Leacroft, Richard, *The Development of the English Playhouse*, 1973.

Lees-Milne, James, *The Earls of Creation*, 1962.

Loftis, John, *Sheridan and the Drama of Georgian England*, Oxford, 1976.

Logan, Olive, 'The Secret Regions of the Stage', *Harper's New Monthly Magazine*, XLVIII (1874), 628–42.

Lynham, Deryck, *The Chevalier Noverre*, 1972.

Mackenzie, Henry, *An Account of the Life and Writings of John Home, Esq.*, Edinburgh, 1822.

Macready, William, *The Reminiscences of William Macready*, ed. Frederick Pollock, 1875.

Mander, Raymond and Mitchenson, Joe, *Guide to the Maugham Collection of Theatrical Paintings*, 1980.

Mammen, Edward William, *The Old Stock Company School of Acting*, Boston, 1945.

Manvell, Roger, *Sarah Siddons: Portrait of an Actress*, 1976.

Manwaring, Elizabeth Wheeler, *Italian Landscape in Eighteenth Century England,* New York, 1925.

McCarthy, Michael, *The Origins of the Gothic Revival*, New Haven and London, 1987.

Mead, William Edward, *The Grand Tour in the Eighteenth Century*, Cambridge, 1914.

Monk, Samuel H., *The Sublime. A Study of Critical Theories in Eighteenth-Century England*, Michigan, 1960.

Moritz, Carl Phillipp, *Travels of Carl Phillipp Moritz*, ed. P. E. Matheson, 1924.

Nicoll, Allardyce, *A History of Late Eighteenth Century Drama*, 1927.

Oulton, Walley Chamberlain, *A History of the Theatres of London*, 1818.

Pascal, Roy, *The German 'Sturm und Drang'*, Manchester, 1953.

Peacock, Thomas Love, *Nightmare Abbey*, 1818, ed. Raymond Wright, 1979.

Pevsner, Nikolaus, 'Richard Payne Knight', *Art Bulletin*, XXI (1949), 293–320.

Praz, Mario, *The Romantic Agony*, 1970.

Pyne, W. H., *Wine and Walnuts*, 1823.

Quennell, Peter, *Romantic England. Writing and Painting, 1717–1851*, 1970.

Radcliffe, Ann, *The Mysteries of Udolpho*, 1794, ed. Bonamy Dobrée, 1980.

Railo, Eino, *The Haunted Castle*, 1927.

Rees, Abraham, ed., *The Cyclopaedia or Universal Dictionary of Arts, Sciences and Literature*, 1803–19.

Rees, Terence, *Theatre Lighting in the Age of Gas*, 1978.

Revels History of Drama in English, 1750–1880, The, ed. Clifford Leech and T. W. Craik.

Reynolds, Joshua, *Discourses on Art*, ed. Robert R. Wark, New Haven, 1975.

Robinson, Henry Crabb, *The London Theatre.* 1811–66, ed. Eluned Brown, 1966.

Robson, William, *The Old Play-Goer*, 1845.

Rosenfeld, Sybil, *Georgian Scene Painters and Scene Painting*, Cambridge, 1981.

'Scene Designs of William Capon', *Theatre Notebook*, X (1955–56), 118–22.

Rosenfeld, Sybil and Croft-Murray, Edward, 'A Checklist of Scene Painters working in Great Britain and Ireland in the Eighteenth Century', *Theatre Notebook*, XIX (1964–65), 6–20, 49–64, 102–13, 133–45, XX (1965–66), 36–44, 69–72, 113–18.

Saint, Andrew, *et al*, *A History of the Royal Opera House, Covent Garden, 1732–1982*, 1982.

Siddons, Henry, *Practical Illustrations of Rhetorical Gesture and Action*, 1807.

Sinko, Grzegorz, *Sheridan and Kotzebue*, Wroclaw, 1949.

Southern, Richard, 'Trick Work in the English Theatre', *Life and Letters To-day*, XXI (1939), 94–100.

Speaight, George, *The History of the English Toy Theatre*, second edn., 1969.

'Stage Storms', *All the Year Round*, VIII (1872), 304–8.

Sterne, Lawrence, *A Sentimental Journey*, 1768, ed. Graham Petrie, 1967.

Stockdale, John Joseph, *The Covent Garden Journal*, 1810.

Stokoe, F. W., *German Influence in the English Romantic Period*, Cambridge, 1926.

Stone, G. W. and Hogan, C. Beecher, *The London Stage*, Parts IV and V, Carbondale, 1962–68.

Stone, William, *The Beauties of the Stage*, 1792.

Summers, Montague, *The Gothic Quest*, 1938.

Survey of London, general editor F. H. W. Sheppard, XXXV: *The Theatre Royal Drury Lane and the Royal Opera House, Covent Garden*, 1970.

Thomas, Graham Stuart, *The Gardens of the National Trust*, 1979.

Thomas, Russell, 'Contemporary Taste in the Stage Decorations of London Theatres, 1770–1800', *Modern Philology*, XLII (1944), 65–79.

Thorp, Willard, 'The Stage Adventures of some Gothic Novels', *Publications of the Modern Language Association of America*, XLIII (1928), 476–86.

Tragedy of Douglas Analysed, The, 1757.

Varma, Devendra P., *The Gothic Flame*, 1957.

Walpole, Horace, *The Castle of Otranto*, 1764, ed. Wilmarth Sheldon Lewis, 1969.

The Yale Edition of Horace Walpole's Correspondence, ed. Wilmarth Sheldon Lewis, 1937–80.

Watkin, David, *The English Vision*, 1982.

Wells, Mitchell, 'Spectacular Scenic Effects of the Eighteenth Century Pantomime', *Philological Quarterly*, XVII (1938), 67–81.

Williams, John Ambrose, *Memoirs of John Philip Kemble*, Esq., 1817.

Woodbury, Lael J., 'Death on the Romantic Stage', *Quarterly Journal of Speech*, XLIX (1963), 57–61.

Wyndham, Henry Saxe, *The Annals of Covent Garden Theatre*, 1906.

Young, M. J., *Memoirs of Mrs Crouch*, 1806.

2. NEWSPAPERS AND JOURNALS

British Review
Critical Review
Dramatic Censor
European Magazine
Examiner
Gazetteer
London Chronicle
Monthly Mirror
Monthly Review
Monthly Visitor
Morning Chronicle
Morning Herald
Morning Post
Prompter
Public Advertiser
Quarterly Review
St James' Chronicle
Theatrical Inquisitor
Thespian Magazine
The Times
Town and Country Magazine
True Briton

3. MANUSCRIPT SOURCES

Bodleian Library, Oxford, Department of Western Manuscripts: Notes on John Henderson's and John Philip Kemble's acting, Ms Douce c 11 f.53.

British Library, London, Department of Manuscripts: Account Books of the Theatre Royal, Covent Garden, B.L. Mss. Eq. 2283–7.

Memoranda of John Philip Kemble, B.L. Addl. Mss. 31972–4. Receipts of Performances at Drury Lane Theatre, 1772–1818, B.M. Addl. Mss. 29709–29711.

4. UNPUBLISHED THESES

Adelsperger, Walter Charles, 'Aspects of the Staging of Plays of the Gothic Revival in England', Ohio State University, 1959.

Hanawalt, L. L., 'The Rise of Gothic Drama, 1765–1800', University of Michigan, 1929.

Jarrett, David, '"Gothic" as a term in Literary Criticism in the Eighteenth Century', University of Oxford, 1968.

McClamroch, Roland, 'The Gothic Drama', University of Northern Carolina, 1927.

McMahon, Patricia M., 'The Tragical Art of Sarah Siddons', University of Yale, 1972.

Miesle, Frank Leland, 'The Staging of Pantomime Entertainments on the London Stage: 1715–1808', Ohio State University, 1955.

Powers, Harvey Marcellus, 'The Theatrical Criticism of Arthur Murphy, Leigh Hunt and William Hazlitt: A Study in changing Taste', Cornell University, 1968.

Preston, Lillian Elvira, 'Phillipe Jacques de Loutherbourg: Eighteenth Century Romantic Artist and Scene Designer', University of Florida, 1957.

5. COLLECTIONS

British Library, London, Department of Manuscripts: Bellamy, B. P., Collection of playbills, 1768–1835, B.L. Addl. Mss. 18590.

Winston, James, Theatrical Collection, Addl. Mss. 38607.

British Library, London, Department of Printed Books: 'Dramatic Notes', B.L. 27831.

Playbills, 93 b. 1; 937 b. 3; 937 f. 2.

Reed, Isaac, 'A Collection of Dramatic Notes', B.L. 25390.

Smith, Richard John, 'Collections for a History of the English Stage', B.L. 38620.

Winston, James, 'A Collection of cuttings, mainly from newspapers, relating to the Theatre Royal, Drury Lane', C. 120 h. 1.

Winston, James, 'A collection of newspaper cuttings relating to the theatres of London', Th. Ctgs. 38–43.

British Museum, London, Print Room:

Grieve, John Henderson, 'Twenty-five Designs for Stage Scenery, some for Covent Garden, others for Astley's', 200+ c 7.

Hamilton, Mary, 'Mrs Siddon's [sic] Dresses and Attitudes in various characters', 201 b 10.

West, W. *et al*, 'Scenes and Figures for Toy Theatres', 168+ a 1–6 b. 1.

Hereford Museum and Art Gallery:
'Collection of engravings of David Garrick; Sarah Siddons and other members of the Kemble family in a variety of roles'.
Hereford Public Library, Local History Collection:
Scrapbooks of the Kemble and Siddons papers.
Theatre Museum, London:
Stone Collection.

6. PROMPT BOOKS

Folger Shakespeare Library, Washington:
Sheridan, Richard Brinsley, *Pizarro*, 1799, Drury Lane, 24 May 1799, P.B. 46.
Theatre Museum, London:
Holcroft, Thomas, *A Tale of Mystery*, 1813, Drury Lane, 4 December 1817, P.B. 203, D.L.
Home, John, *Douglas*, n.d., Drury Lane, 6 May 1818.
Lewis, Matthew Gregory, *The Castle Spectre*, 1803, Drury Lane, 28 November 1833, P.B. 28 D.L.
Murphy, Arthur, *The Grecian Daughter*, n.d., Drury Lane, 3 May 1813, P.B. 48 D.L.

Appendix One: A Chronological List of the First Performances of Gothic Plays, 1750–1820.

The following list gives the date of the first night of major gothic plays performed at the Theatre Royal, Covent Garden (C.G.), the Theatre Royal, Drury Lane (D.L.) and the Haymarket Theatre (H). Where appropriate the first night date and location is given of a few plays which opened in cities other than London before a transfer took place. The more important gothic dramas which were staged solely at non-London theatres or the minor metropolitan playhouses are also included.

The list given in Bertrand Evans's publication, *Gothic Drama from Walpole to Shelley*, was a useful starting point. This contains some inaccuracies, however, and omits certain plays which reasonably may be included. *The London Stage*, a hand-book not available to Evans, was a useful source of verification.

Play	Author	Theatre	First Night
Douglas	John Home	Edinburgh	14 December 1756
		C.G.	14 March 1757
The Countess of Salisbury	Hall Hartson	Dublin	2 May 1765
		H.	31 August 1767
Almida	Dorothea Celesia	D.L.	1 January 1771
The Grecian Daughter	Arthur Murphy	D.L.	26 February 1772
Eldred	John Jackson	Dublin	2 December 1773
		H.	7 July 1775
The Heroine of the Cave	Paul Hifferman	D.L.	19 March 1774
Braganza	Robert Jephson	D.L.	17 February 1775
Percy	Hannah More	C.G.	10 December 1777
The British Heroine	John Jackson	C.G.	5 May 1778
The Law of Lombardy	Robert Jephson	D.L.	2 August 1779

175

The Fatal Falsehood	Hannah More	C.G.	6 May 1779
Albina, Countess of Raimond	Hannah Cowley	H.	31 July 1779
Zoraida	William Hodson	D.L.	13 December 1779
The Count of Narbonne	Robert Jephson	C.G.	17 November 1781
Banditti	John O'Keeffe	C.G.	28 November 1781
The Castle of Andalusia	John O'Keeffe	C.G.	2 November 1782
The Mysterious Husband	Richard Cumberland	C.G.	28 January 1783
Lord Russell	William Hayley	H.	18 August 1784
The Carmelite	Richard Cumberland	D.L.	2 December 1784
The Nunnery	William Pearce	C.G.	12 April 1785
Richard, Coeur-de-Lion	John Burgoyne	D.L.	5 October 1786
Richard, Coeur-de-Lion	Leonard MacNally	C.G.	16 October 1786
The Enchanted Castle	Miles Peter Andrews	C.G.	26 December 1786
Julia	Robert Jephson	D.L.	14 April 1787
Vimonda	Andrew McDonald	H.	5 September 1787
The Regent	Bertie Greatheed	D.L.	29 March 1788
The Battle of Hexham	George Colman the Younger	H.	11 August 1789
The Haunted Tower	James Cobb	D.L.	24 November 1789
The Crusade	Frederick Reynolds	C.G.	6 May 1790
Lorenzo	Robert Merry	C.G.	5 April 1791
The Kentish Barons	Francis North	H.	25 June 1791
The Midnight Wanderers	William Pearce	C.G.	25 February 1793
The Ward of the Castle	Miss Burke	C.G.	24 October 1793
The Travellers in Switzerland	Henry Bate [Dudley]	C.G.	25 February 1794
Fountainville Forest	James Boaden	C.G.	25 March 1794
Netley Abbey	William Pearce	C.G.	10 April 1794
The Sicilian Romance	Henry Siddons	C.G.	28 May 1794
Lodoiska	John Philip Kemble	D.L.	9 June 1794
The Apparition	James Cross	H.	3 September 1794
The Mysteries of the Castle	Miles Peter Andrews	C.G.	31 January 1795

176

The Adopted Child	Samuel Birch	D.L.	1 May 1795
The Secret Tribunal	James Boaden	C.G.	3 June 1795
The Iron Chest	George Colman the Younger	D.L.	12 March 1796
The Days of Yore	Richard Cumberland	C.G.	13 January 1796
Almeyda, Queen of Granada	Sophia Lee	D.L.	20 April 1796
Don Pedro	Richard Cumberland	H.	23 July 1796
The Italian Monk	James Boaden	H.	15 August 1797
The Castle Spectre	Matthew Gregory Lewis	D.L.	14 December 1797
Raymond and Agnes	Charles Farley	C.G.	16 March 1797
Blue-Beard	George Colman the Younger	D.L.	16 January 1798
The Inquisitor	Thomas Holcroft	H.	23 June 1798
The Cambro-Britons	James Boaden	H.	21 July 1798
The Outlaws	Andrew Franklin	D.L.	16 October 1798
Albert and Adelaide	Samuel Birch	C.G.	11 December 1798
Aurelio and Miranda	James Boaden	D.L.	29 December 1798
Feudal Times	George Colman the Younger	D.L.	19 January 1799
The Castle of Montval	Thomas Sedgwick Whalley	D.L.	23 April 1799
Pizarro	Richard Brinsley Sheridan	D.L.	24 May 1799
Fortune's Frolic	John Till Allingham	C.G.	25 May 1799
The Castle of Sorrento	Henry Heartwell	H.	13 July 1799
The Red Cross Knights	Joseph Holman	H.	21 August 1799
De Monfort	Joanna Baillie	D.L.	29 April 1800
Julian and Agnes	William Sotheby	D.L.	25 April 1801
Adelmorn the Outlaw	Matthew Gregory Lewis	D.L.	4 May 1801
Alfonso, King of Castile	Matthew Gregory Lewis	C.G.	15 January 1802
The Tale of Mystery	Thomas Holcroft	C.G.	13 November 1802
The Harper's Daughter	Matthew Gregory Lewis	C.G.	4 May 1803
A Tale of Terror	Henry Siddons	C.G.	12 May 1803
The Maid of Bristol	James Boaden	H.	24 August 1803

Valentine and Orson	Thomas John Dibdin	C.G.	3 April 1804
The Hunter of the Alps	William Dimond	H.	3 July 1804
Foul Deeds Will Rise	Samuel Arnold	H.	18 July 1804
The Venetian Outlaw	Robert William Elliston	D.L.	26 April 1805
Rugantino	Matthew Gregory Lewis	C.G.	18 October 1805
Adrian and Orrila	William Dimond	C.G.	15 November 1806
Edgar	George Manners	C.G.	9 May 1806
Alberto and Lauretta	Thomas J. Lynch	H.	15 December 1806
The Curfew	John Tobin	D.L.	19 February 1807
One O'Clock	Matthew Gregory Lewis	D.L.	1 April 1807
Adelgitha	Matthew Gregory Lewis	D.L.	30 April 1807
Ella Rosenberg	James Kenney	D.L.	19 November 1807
The Blind Boy	James Kenney	C.G.	1 December 1807
Faulkner	William Godwin	D.L.	16 December 1807
Boniface and Bridgetina	Thomas John Dibdin	C.G.	31 March 1808
The Mysterious Bride	Lumley St. George Skeffington	D.L.	1 June 1808
The Forest of Hermanstadt	Thomas John Dibdin	C.G.	7 October 1808
The Exile	Frederick Reynolds	C.G.	10 November 1808
Venoni	Matthew Gregory Lewis	D.L.	1 December 1808
The Foundling of the Forest	William Dimond	H.	10 July 1809
Raymond and Agnes	Matthew Gregory Lewis	Norwich	22 November 1809
The Free Knights	Frederick Reynolds	C.G.	8 February 1810
The Lady of the Lake	Thomas John Dibdin	S.	24 September 1810
The Lady of the Lake	Edmund St. John Eyre	Edinburgh	15 January 1811
Timour the Tartar	Matthew Gregory Lewis	C.G.	29 April 1811
The Quadrupeds of Quedinburgh	George Colman the Younger	L	18 July 1811
		H.	26 July 1811

The House of Morville	John Lake	L.	27 February 1812
The Devil's Bridge	Samuel James Arnold	L.	6 May 1812
Look at Home	Edmund St. John Eyre	H.	15 August 1812
The Aethiop	William Dimond	C.G.	6 October 1812
Remorse	Samuel Taylor Coleridge	D.L.	23 January 1813
The Miller and his Men	Isaac Pocock	C.G.	21 October 1813
The Wandering Boys	John Kerr	C.G.	24 February 1814
The Orphan of the Castle	William Dimond	Bath	17 March 1814
The Woodman's Hut	Samuel James Arnold	D.L.	12 April 1814
Bobinet the Bandit	anon.	C.G.	4 December 1815
Bertram	Charles Robert Maturin	D.L.	9 May 1816
The Broken Sword	William Dimond	C.G.	7 October 1816
Manuel	Charles Robert Maturin	D.L.	8 March 1817
The Conquest of Taranto	William Dimond	C.G.	15 April 1817
The Apostate	Robert Lalor Sheil	C.G.	3 May 1817
The Falls of Clyde	George Soane	D.L.	8 October 1817
The Bridge of Abydos	William Dimond	D.L.	5 February 1818
Evadne	Robert Lalor Sheil	C.G.	10 February 1819
The Ruffian Boy	Thomas John Dibdin	S.	15 February 1819
The Italians	Charles Bucke	D.L.	8 April 1819
Fredolpho	Charles Robert Maturin	C.G.	12 May 1819
The Bridge of Lammermoor	Thomas John Dibdin	S.	5 July 1819
Montoni	Robert Lalor Sheil	C.G.	3 May 1820

Appendix Two: Biographical Glossary

AICKIN, Francis (died 1805), actor at Drury Lane and Covent Garden; Francis Godolphin Waldron commented on his lack of taste in stage costume.

AIKIN, John (1747–1822), physician in Yarmouth and London; man of letters.

ALLINGHAM, John Till (flourished 1799–1810), writer of comedies and farces.

ANDREWS, Miles Peter (died 1814), Member of Parliament; established spectacular entertainments at his house in Green Park, London; playwright.

BAILLIE, Joanna (1762–1851), poet and dramatist whose work gained commendation from Sir Walter Scott.

BARBAULD, Anna Letitia (1743–1845), poet and essayist.

BARRETT, Giles Linnett (1744–1809), a much travelled performer, sometime manager of the Norwich theatre.

BARRY, Spranger (1719–77), Irish actor; leading player at Drury Lane and Covent Garden.

BARRYMORE, William (1759–1830), actor at Drury Lane; specialised in the role of the villain.

BEATTIE, James (1735–1803), professor of moral philosophy at Aberdeen; poet.

BECKFORD, William (1759–1844), builder of Fonthill Abbey, Wiltshire and Lansdown Tower, Bath; author of the gothic novel, *Vathek* (1786); traveller and diarist.

BERNARD, John (1756–1828), actor, manager and author.

BETTY, William Henry West (1791–1847), juvenile performer who won great acclaim; attempts to establish himself as an actor in later life failed.

BIGGS, Anne (1775–1825), Mrs Samuel Young, actress and singer at Bath and Drury Lane.

BLAIR, Hugh (1718–1800), cleric; professor of rhetoric at Edinburgh.

BOADEN, James (1762–1839), editor of the *Oracle*; biographer of numbers of Georgian stage performers; occasional playwright.

BOOTH the Elder, Junius Brutus (1796–1852), tragic actor; rival to Edmund Kean; emigrated to New York in 1821.

BROWN, John (1715–66), cleric; occasional poet and playwright; essayist.

BURGOYNE, John (1722–92), British General in the Seven Years War and the War of American Independence; playwright.

BURNS, Robert (1759–96), poet and songwriter; farmer.

BUSBY, Thomas (1755–1838), organist at several London churches; composer and theatre musician.

BYRON, George Gordon (1788–1824), aristocrat; poet and verse dramatist; member of the Drury Lane committee of management from 1815.

CABANEL, Rudolph (1762–1839), machinist; employed in the construction of Drury Lane, the Royal Circus and the Coburg.

CAMP, Maria Theresa de (1775–1832), Mrs Charles Kemble, actress at Drury Lane and the Haymarket.

CAMPBELL, Thomas (1777–1844), poet; editor of the *New Monthly Magazine* and the *Metropolitan Magazine*.

CANNING, George (1770–1827), statesman and orator; co-author of the satirical play, *The Rovers*, published 1798 and performed the following year.

CAPON, William (1765–1827), easel and scenic artist; worked at Drury Lane and the English Opera House; mediaeval architectural historian.

CARTER, John (1748–1817), architectural draughtsman; wrote a series of letters to the *Gentleman's Magazine* criticising the restoration of mediaeval buildings, signing himself, 'An Architect'.

CHAMBERS, Sir William (1726–96), architect, designer of Somerset House, London; traveller.

COBB, James (1756–1818), secretary, East India Company; prolific writer of operettas, farces and comedies.

COLMAN the Younger, George (1762–1836), playwright; sometime manager of Covent Garden; Examiner of Plays.

COOKE, George Frederick (1756–1812), gifted tragic actor; often inebriated.

COWLEY, Hannah (1743–1809), playwright; writer of sentimental verse.

COXE, William (1747–1828), cleric; rector of Bemerton, Wiltshire; historian; travel writer.

CRADOCK, Joseph (1742–1826), author of several tragedies; promoter of private theatricals in Leicester.

CRAWFORD, Ann (1734–1801), previously Ann Dancer; played at Covent Garden under the later name after the death of her actor husband, Spranger Barry.

CROUCH, Anna Maria (1763–1805), soprano singer and actress; intimate of Michael Kelly.

CUMBERLAND, Richard (1732–1811), sentimental dramatist; figured in Sheridan's satire *The Critic* as Sir Fretful Plagiary.

DASHWOOD, Sir Francis (1701–81), Chancellor of the Exchequer (1762–63) in Lord Bute's government; founder member of a number of societies amongst which were the Dilettanti and the Divan Club; another group, the Monks of Medmenham, later met in his home village of West Wycombe.

DELANY, Mary (1700–88), née Granville; conversationalist and letter writer; friend of George III.

DIBDIN, Thomas (1771–1841), actor, songwriter, scene-painter and playwright.

DIMOND, William (?1780-?1836), playwright; writer of operettas.

DUTTON, Thomas (flourished 1798), writer and editor; his few works concentrate on the London stage.

DYER, John (1699–1758), cleric; incumbent of several Lincolnshire parishes; poet; sometime itinerant artist in Wales.

ELLIS, George (1753–1815), contributor to the Tory newspaper, the *Anti-Jacobin*.

ELLISTON, Robert William (1774–1831), actor; playwright; manager of Drury Lane and the Surrey.

FARLEY, Charles (1771–1859), actor and dancer painted by De Wilde; acting manager in charge of pantomimes and ballet at Covent Garden until his retirement in 1834.

FITZGERALD, Percy (1834–1925), novelist; biographer; writer on the stage.

FRERE, John Hookham (1769–1846), diplomatist and author.

FUSELI, Henry (1741–1825), professor of painting at the Royal Academy from 1799 until his death; created fearful visionary paintings.

GALT, John (1779–1839), poet, novelist and essayist; traveller.

GARRICK, David (1717–79), actor; playwright; manager of Drury Lane (1747–1776); stage reformer.

GENEST, John (1764–1839), cleric; curate in Lincolnshire; retired because of ill health to Bath where he compiled his history of the English stage.

GIFFORD, William (1756–1826), translator of classical authors; satirist.

GILPIN, William (1724–1804), vicar of Boldre in the New Forest; aesthetic theorist with a consuming passion for the picturesque.

GLUCK, Christopher (1714–87), German composer; writer of operas.

GOLDSMITH, Oliver (1730–74), poet and playwright; enemy of the sentimental drama.

GRAVES, Richard (1715–1804), rector of Claverton, Bath; author of the novel *The Spiritual Quixote* (1773).

GRAY, Thomas (1716–71), Poet Laureate; professor of history and modern languages at Cambridge; letter writer.

GREATHEED, Bertie (1759–1826), of Guy's Cliffe, Warwick, where he made considerable improvements; writer.

GREENWOOD the Elder, Thomas (flourished 1772–1797), scene-painter at Drury Lane from 1772 until his death.

GREENWOOD the Younger, Thomas (flourished 1779–1822), succeeded his father, Thomas Greenwood the Elder, as scene-painter at Drury Lane.

GRIEVE, John Henderson (1770–1845), scene-painter at Covent Garden.

HAMILTON, William (1751–1801), painter of literary subjects.

HARRIS, Thomas (died 1820), manager of Covent Garden from 1774 until his death.

HARTSON, Hall (died 1773), other than his play, *The Countess of Salisbury*, he attempted little writing.

HAYDON, Benjamin Robert (1786–1846), historical painter; promoter of government patronage of the arts.

HENDERSON, John (1747–85), actor; played at Bath, the Haymarket and the patent houses.

HOARE, Sir Richard Colt (1758–1838), Wiltshire historian; improver of Stourhead.

HOLCROFT, Thomas (1745–1809), playwright and translator of French and Spanish dramas.

HOLLAND, Henry (?1746–1806), architect; noted for his work at Drury Lane and at Carlton House, London.

HOLMAN, Joseph (1764–1817), London actor and playwright.

HOME, John (1722–1808), Scottish clergyman, removed from his ministry after the success of his play *Douglas*; secretary to Lord Bute.

HUME, David (1711–76), philosopher, historian and essayist.

HUNT, Leigh (1784–1859), poet, essayist and critic; editor of the *Examiner*.

INCHBALD, Elizabeth (1753–1821), actress, dramatist, editor of collections of plays, novelist.

JACKSON, Hester (1751–1806), tragic actress; wife of the Scottish manager John Jackson; first performed the role of Lady Randolph at Covent Garden in 1779.

JEPHSON, Robert (1736–1803), satirist and playwright; dramatised Horace Walpole's novel *The Castle of Otranto* under the title of *The Count of Narbonne*.

JOHNSON, Samuel (1709–84), writer and lexicographer.

JOHNSTON, Alexander (died 1810), machinist and costume designer at Drury Lane from 1789 until his death.

JOHNSTONE, Ann (flourished 1797–1807), later Mrs Charles Presbury; a performer in the 'Siddons tradition' at Bath and Drury Lane.

JOMMELLI, Niccolo (1714–74), Neapolitan composer.

JORDAN, Dorothea (1761–1816), ebullient actress who specialised in transvestite roles in her younger days; mistress of the Duke of Clarence; returned to the stage when he became King William IV.

KEAN, Edmund (1787/90–1833), tragic actor.

KEATS, John (1795–1821), poet; many works embody gothic themes and settings.

KELLY, Frances Maria (1790–1882), performer at Drury Lane; founder of a school for actresses.

KELLY, Michael (1762–1826), Irish tenor, actor and composer; acting manager of the King's Theatre.

KEMBLE, John Philip (1757–1823), brother of Sarah Siddons; actor and acting manager of Drury Lane and Covent Garden; playwright.

KERR, John (flourished 1801–45), playwright.

KNIGHT, Sir Richard Payne (1750–1824), traveller; improver of Downton, Worcester and Herefordshire; writer on a wide range of philosophical and literary topics.

KOTZEBUE, August von (1761–1819), sentimental German dramatist whose works were much translated into English in the latter part of the eighteenth century.

LAKE, John (flourished 1812–15), author of *The House of Morville* and *The Golden Grove*.

LAWRENCE, Sir Thomas (1769–1830), courtly and elegant portrait painter.

LEE, Sophia (1750–1824), novelist and dramatist.

LENNOX, Lord William Pitt (1799–1881), military man; sportsman; performer at private theatricals; miscellaneous writer.

LEWIS, Matthew Gregory (1775–1818), author of the novel *The Monk* (1796) and writer of numerous gothic dramas.

LORRAINE, Claude (1600–82), landscape painter, born Nancy, worked in Naples and Rome.

LOUTHERBOURG, Philippe Jacques de (1740–1812), scenic designer under Garrick and Sheridan at Drury Lane; devised the model mechanical theatre, the Eidophusikon, at Leicester Square.

LUPINO, Thomas Frederick (?1749-?1845), scene-painter at Drury Lane and Covent Garden.

MACDONALD, Andrew (?1755–90), his only success as a playwright was with *Vimonda*, staged in London and Edinburgh.

MACNALLY, Leonard (1752–1820), lawyer; poet ('Sweet Lass of Richmond Hill'); pamphleteer.

MACPHERSON, James (1736–96), Scottish writer; promoter of Ossian's poetry; when asked to produce the original manuscripts he fabricated the material.

MACREADY, William (1793–1873), tragic actor; manager of Drury Lane and Covent Garden.

MAHON, Robert (1737–99), member of an Irish theatrical family; played in Dublin and Covent Garden.

MALTON, Thomas (1748–1804), architectural painter; wrote a treatise on the craft of perspective drawing.

MANNERS, George (1778–1853), lawyer; British consul at Boston; editor of the *Satirist*; playwright.,

MARINARI, Gaetano (flourished 1764–1844), painter and machinist at Drury Lane, the Haymarket, the King's and the Royalty.

MASON, William (1725–97), canon and precentor of York Minster; writer on gardening and painting; garden designer.

MATURIN, Charles Robert (1784–1819), impoverished Dublin clergyman; writer of romances and plays.

MORITZ, Carl Philipp (1756–93), cleric; unsuccessful actor; writer on language and psychology; teacher.

MURPHY, Arthur (1727–1805), playwright; theatre critic for the *London Chronicle* for two years from 1757.

NOVERRE, Jean Georges (1727–1809), choreographer; sometime maitre-de-ballet of the Opera Comique, Paris.

O'KEEFFE, John (1747–1833), actor and playwright; his comedy, *Wild Oats*, is well-known today.

PALMER, John (1728–68), actor known as 'Gentleman Palmer' because of his aristocratic but stiff carriage.

PARK, Arthur (1818–80), free-lance artist and engraver; established a family printing business at Lambeth and in the City.

PASQUIN, Anthony, the pen name of John Williams.

PEARCE, William (flourished 1785–95), writer of light operas.

PIOZZI, Hester (1741–1821), née Thrale; resident of Streatham Park; letter writer.

PIRANESI, Giovanni (1720–78), architect; etched many of the ruins of Roman antiquity in which he exploited contrasts of light and shade.

PLUMPTRE, Anne (1760–1818), writer on eighteenth-century German literature.

POCOCK, Isaac (1782–1835), prolific playwright.

POPE, Alexander (1688–1744), poet who used the metaphor of the theatre in his work; garden designer.

POUSSIN, Nicolas (1594–1665), artist, worked in Paris and Rome.

POWELL, Mary Ann (flourished 1790), actress.

PUGH, Charles (flourished 1786–1828), scene-painter at the Lyceum and the patent houses.

RADCLIFFE, Ann (1764–1823), writer of gothic romances; poet.

RAE, Alexander (1782–1820), actor; stage-manager at Drury Lane.

REEVE, Clara (1729–1807), novelist; she gained some fame with her gothic novel *The Old English Baron*.

REIN, Mary (flourished 1790–1800), costume designer at Drury Lane.

REPTON, Humphrey (1752–1818), designer of informal landscape gardens; noted for his 'red books' in which he presented his suggestions to his clients.

REYNOLDS, Frederick (1764–1841) author of many spectacular plays.

REYNOLDS, Sir Joshua (1723–93), highly popular portrait painter; first President of the Royal Academy of Arts.

RICHARDS, John Inigo (flourished 1751–1810), scene-painter at Covent Garden.

RIVERS, Mrs (died 1832), née Ranoe; actress at York and Edinburgh.

ROBINSON, Henry Crabb (1755–1867), foreign editor of *The Times*; barrister, diarist and intrepid theatre-goer.

ROGERS, Samuel (1763–1855), traveller; man of letters; conversationalist.

ROOKER, Michael Angelo (1746–1801), landscape artist; scene designer at the Haymarket.

ROSA, Salvator (1615–73), Neapolitan painter of wild landscapes; his work was highly collectable in the eighteenth century and popular with gothic writers.

SCHILLER, Friedrich von (1759–1805), playwright; poet; the chief figure of the 'Sturm und Drang' (Storm and Stress) literary movement.

SEWARD, Anna (1747–1809), poet, essayist and correspondent; domiciled in Lichfield and known as the 'Swan of Lichfield'; invalid.

SHERIDAN, Richard Brinsley (1751–1816), playwright; manager of Drury Lane (1776–1809); Whig politician.

SIDDONS, Henry (1775–1815), son of Sarah, indifferent actor at the Theatre Royal, Edinburgh.

SIDDONS, Sarah (1755–1831), sister of John Philip Kemble; English tragic actress of the highest repute.

SKELT, Matthew and Ben (flourished 1840–50), members of a family business founded by Martin Skelt, producing toy theatre scenes and figures.

SOANE, George (1790–1860), playwright, novelist and biographer.

SOTHEBY, William (1757–1833), prominent figure in London literary circles; classical scholar, antiquarian and poet.

STERNE, Laurence (1713–68), novelist; perpetual curate of Coxwold, Yorkshire.

TALBOT, Montagu (1774–1831), travelling actor; appeared in Dublin and London as well as the provinces.

TAYLOR, John (1757–1832), occulist to George III; dramatic critic.

THACKERAY, William Makepeace (1811–63), novelist and editor.

THOMSON, James (1834–82), poet, chiefly remembered for 'The City of Dreadful Night' (1874).

THORNTON, Henry (1750–1818), provincial theatre manager working in the home counties and along the south coast.

TROTTER, Thomas (1779–1851), theatre manager in Kent and Sussex; based for much of his professional life at Worthing.

TURNER, Joseph Mallord William (1775–1851), landscape artist; often drawing on gothic motifs, he influenced the late Georgian notion of the sublime.

WALPOLE, Horace (1717–97), traveller; garden enthusiast; essayist; letter writer; designer of Strawberry Hill.

WARNER, Richard (1763–1857), curate of Boldre, Hampshire and of St James', Bath; man of letters and antiquarian.

WEBB, William (flourished 1844–90), printer, specialising in theatrical portraits and toy theatre sheets; worked in Bermondsey and the City.

WEST, William (1811–54), printer of toy theatre sheets; based in the Strand area.

WILKINSON, Tate (1739–1803), manager of the York circuit; autobiographer.

WILLIAMS, John (1761–1818), poet, biographer and satirist; sometimes wrote under the *nom-de-plume*, 'Anthony Pasquin'.

WOFFINGTON, Margaret (1718–60), known as 'Peg'; leading actress at the patent houses.

YATES, Mary Ann (1728–87), tragic actress at Drury Lane from 1754 until 1785.

YOUNG, Charles Mayne (1777–1856), actor; disciple of Kemble.

Index

Excluding Play Titles

The notes and appendices are not included in the indexes.

Index

Index

Index of Play Titles

Index of Play Titles